New Kittredge Shakespeare

William Shakespeare

THE MERCHANT OF VENICE

William Shakespeare

THE MERCHANT OF VENICE

Editor
Kenneth S. Rothwell
Emeritus Professor,
University of Vermont

Series Editor
James H. Lake
Louisiana State University,
Shreveport

For Bev

Edited by George Lyman Kittredge.
Used with permission from the heirs to the Kittredge estate.

Cover Design by Guy Wetherbee | Elk Amino Design, New England | elkaminodesign.com

Cover illustration by Averil Burleigh for *The Merchant of Venice: Told by a Popular Novelist* (John C. Winston Company, 1914).

ISBN: 978-1-58510-264-8
ISBN 10: 1-58510-264-4

10 9 8 7 6 5 4 3 2 1

0208TS

TABLE OF CONTENTS

Publisher's Note

George Lyman Kittredge's insightful editions of Shakespeare have endured in part because of his eclecticism, his diversity of interests, and his wide-ranging accomplishments — all of which are reflected in the valuable notes in each volume. The plays in the *New Kittredge Shakespeare* series retain the original Kittredge notes and introductions, changed or augmented only when some modernization seems necessary. These new editions also include introductory essays by contemporary editors, notes on the plays as they have been performed on stage and film, and additional student materials.

These plays are being made available by Focus Publishing with the permission of the Kittredge heirs.

Ron Pullins, Publisher
Newburyport, 2007

Acknowledgments

I am grateful to Ron Pullins and James H. Lake, and to Amanda Pepper and Cindy Zawalich as well as to the staff of the University of Vermont library, for helping me through the intricacies of producing this book.

Kenneth S. Rothwell
December 2007

INTRODUCTION TO THE KITTREDGE EDITION[1]

THE MERCHANT OF VENICE was entered in the Stationers' Register on July 22, 1598 ("a booke of the Marchaunt of Venyce, or otherwise called the Jewe of Venyce"), and again (without the alternative title) on October 28, 1600.[2] In 1600 the First Quarto appeared, the basis for both the present edition and the text in the 1623 Folio. Presumably, the date of composition would be 1596.

Most of the plot comes in some fashion from the story of Giannetto, in *Il Pecorone* of Ser Giovanni Fiorentino (4.1) which dates from the last quarter of the fourteenth century but was not printed until 1558. A variation appears in the *Dolopathos* in the Latin *Gesta Romanorum*.

The Pound of Flesh story is also old and has circulated extensively. In the Middle English *Cursor Mundi* it is worked into the legend of the discovery of the True Cross. Shylock's argument in court also has points in common with the Jew's oration in Lazarus Piot's *The Orator* (1596).

The Choice of the Casket comes from the Orient. It had originally nothing to do with winning a wife but was used to illustrate the perverse judgment that prefers show to substance.[3] From the legend of *Barlaam and Joasaph* it was taken in the thirteenth century by Vincent of Beauvais into his *Speculum Historiale* (15. 10), and then into many other variants. A lost drama mentioned by Stephen Gosson, in his famous diatribe against the stage *The School of Abuse* (1579), describes a drama called *The Jew*, "showne at the Bull," as "representing the greedinesse of worldly chusers, and bloody mindes of Usurers." These phrases suggest that the plot anticipated Shakespeare in combining The Choice of the Casket with The Pound of Flesh. If Shakespeare owed anything to *The Jew*, his indebtedness was doubtless limited to

---

1   Kittredge's introduction, a model of painstaking and detailed scholarship, is monumentally thorough in its coverage and deserves careful study. It has been changed very little here and then only to eliminate unfamiliar references. [K.R.]

2   The Stationers' Register served as a kind of copyright office to protect the rights of playwrights and others.

3   A favorite Shakespearean theme is the gap between "appearance vs. reality," which is synonymous with "show vs. substance," or even "you can't tell a book by its cover." In *Hamlet*, the uncle Claudius fits the type of a man who "can smile and smile and be a villain."

the substitution of the caskets for the dramatically unmanageable sleeping potion in the *Il Pecorone* tale

Anthony Munday's usurer's daughter in Part III of his *Zelauto* (1580) shows some resemblances to Shakespeare's Jessica, but perhaps no source for the Jessica episode need be sought beyond the rôle of Marlowe's Abigail in *The Jew of Malta*. That Shakespeare knew Marlowe's tragedy was a matter of course. Its influence is pervasively discernible and there are several points of special contact—in particular, the scene in which the daughter throws the treasure out of the window. But Jessica is not Abigail, and Shylock is not, like Barabas, a Machiavellian villain.

The name *Shylock* is thought to be the Hebrew *shalach,* translated by "cormorant" in *Leviticus,* xi. 17, and *Deuteronomy,* xiv. 17. "Away, thou money-mong'ring cormorant!" says Eutrapelus to the usurer Philargurus in the anonymous play of *Timon* (v.5), which may date from 1590 or earlier. In *Coriolanus* (i.1.125) "the cormorant belly" typifies the patricians who "make edicts for usury, to support usurers." *Jessica* seems to come from *Jesca (Iescha* in the Vulgate), a form of *Iscah,* the name of the daughter of Haran (*Genesis,* xi. 29), interpreted as "she that looketh out." This would fit 2. 5. 29 ff., where Shylock forbids Jessica to "clamber up to the casements" and "thrust her head into the public street to gaze on Christian fools," and Launcelot prompts her to "look out at a window, for all this." Frequently cited also in connection with Shylock is Roderigo Lopez, Queen Elizabeth's physician, a converted Jew, who was accused of plotting to poison her. Though probably innocent, he was horribly executed by hanging, drawing and quartering for high treason on June 7, 1594, but it is hard to see what the Lopez affair has to do with Shakespeare's play (except to contribute to a malaise of anti-Semitism). The character of Shylock fascinates critics and has lured them into endless mazes of debate. One thing is clear, however: THE MERCHANT OF VENICE is no anti-Semitic document; Shakespeare was not attacking the Jewish people when he gave Shylock the villain's rôle. If so, he was attacking the Moors in *Titus Andronicus,* the Spaniards in *Much Ado,* the Italians in *Cymbeline,* the Viennese in *Measure for Measure,* the Danes in *Hamlet,* the Britons in *King Lear,* the Scots in *Macbeth,* and the English in *Richard the Third.*[4]

Editor's Note

Every effort has been made to retain the Kittredge introduction as it was first published. Extremely long and recondite allusions to literary works that may seem irrelevant to today's students have been eliminated. Sentences with more syntactical weight than seems necessary have been revised. Highly abstruse textual problems outside the interest of most undergraduates have also been purged. Explanatory footnotes are mine.

K.S.R.

---

4   Kittredge's spirited denial of anti-Semitic elements was written well before Adolf Hitler's notorious Holocaust, which resulted in the destruction of major cohorts of European Jewry, and ultimately brought about the founding of Israel. More recently scholars have spoken of the play as being *about* anti-Semitism but not intrinsically anti-Semitic.

INTRODUCTION TO THE FOCUS EDITION: PERFORMANCE CONSIDERATIONS AND HISTORY

How Does the Play Work?

Just as Prince Hamlet railed against his false friends, Rosencrantz and Guildenstern, who "would pluck out the heart of [his] mystery," so also his creator, William Shakespeare, spins in his grave as armies of scholars, critics, and directors struggle to ferret out his hidden agendas. With the possible exception of *Hamlet*, *The Merchant of Venice* offers more puzzles, ambiguity, contradictions, problems, and riddles than any of the other plays. Elizabethan audiences, steeped in legendary and mythological lore, may have been oblivious to these problems, but literal-minded twenty-first century readers still find "suspension of belief" more unwilling than willing.

The *Merchant of Venice* tells romantic tales about Venice while a villain, Shylock, like the phantom of the opera, lurks in the background itching to spread unhappiness. Among modern critics, *The Merchant of Venice* has been viewed as an exercise in the conflict between New and Old Testament values (Portia's defense of mercy and Shylock's plea for the letter of the law); as a masterpiece of parallel plots linked by a common concern with "commodity" (the cold-blooded exchange of merchandise); from a "presentist" (or modern point of view), as a snide commentary on the bourgeois false consciousness of the Belmont elite; or as a superb example of Shakespeare's gift for lyric theatre, especially in the fifth act duet between Jessica and Lorenzo; in the post-Holocaust era it has shared with the infamous Protocols of Zion a reputation as a savage exercise in anti-Semitism; and again as a subtle attack on Christian hypocrisy. These issues have been cogently summed up in James Bulman's observation that "*The Merchant* is a play whose potential to be various things at once—allegory and folk tale, romantic comedy and problem play—may have been realizable only on the Elizabethan stage." [1] It has also won the distinction of being the Shakespearean play that has been most frequently threatened with banishment. What is to be made out of this morass of opinion in which truths and half truths create more cacophony than harmony?

The answer is that much can and has been made of this towering but ramshackle verbal edifice. As Kittredge's introduction points out, the play has been seen as comprised of *two* plot lines: the bond and the casket, culled from the prolix sagas of European romance. Anyone reading it, however, soon discovers that this formula is

---

1   *The Merchant of Venice* (Manchester and New York, 1991), p.6.

too reductive to handle the play's tangle of events. Most obviously there is the contrast between the mercantile Venetian plot and the romantic Belmont episodes. There is also the sub-plot on the elopement of Shylock's daughter Jessica with Lorenzo, which sets up parallels between Jessica's and Portia's fathers as tyrannical masculine figures. The exchange of gifts, goods, and especially women enters into the dynamic of the Venetian economy. There is the story of the betrothal rings, in which the rings of Bassanio and Gratiano are sneakily purloined by a disguised Portia and Nerissa. As a sidebar a treacherous Jessica barters away her father's heirloom turquoise ring for a monkey. Somehow in the midst of all these shenanigans, the primary question has always surged around the dominating character of Shylock, who whether seen as villain or victim has tended to push the other characters into the background, so much so that students are exhorted to remember that the "merchant" of Venice is not Shylock but Antonio. Ironically, however, even Portia has trouble distinguishing among characters when in the trial scene she asks "Which is the merchant here? and which the Jew?" (4.1.174).

Shylock stands at the center of the "bond-motive" in which the well meaning Antonio negotiates a loan from Shylock in order to help the penniless Bassanio woo Portia, the lady "richly left" of Belmont. Although it begins in a "merry sport" (1.3.138), Antonio's pledge to Shylock of a pound of flesh as collateral carries ferocious dangers. The literal-minded Shylock is quite capable of turning the joke into a nightmare by insisting, with the backing of strict Venetian law, on an actual rather than a symbolic pound of flesh, "to be cut off and taken/ In what part of your body pleaseth me." Because the part of the body that Shylock has in mind is not immediately revealed, some fertile thinkers have actually wondered if the reference to "cutting off" does not allude to the penis, or even to circumcision, though in the fourth act the "part" turns out to be a chunk of raw flesh alarmingly close to the heart. In the Radford film this outcome is presaged in the Rialto meat market where the peddler holds up a revolting chunk of goat meat. A nearby scale foreshadows Shylock's "balance" in the court room. Exactness is the essence of a business transaction.

Antonio's misfortunes attract a swarm of scheming parasites. Everyone's motives come into question. Is Bassanio, in seeking the money from Antonio, acting out of genuine love for Portia, or out of a base desire to prop up his sagging fortunes? Is he exploiting Antonio for his riches as a shipping magnate, or is there a genuine affection of the young man for the older? Surrounding Bassanio and Antonio is a claque of frivolous cronies, "good old boys," men with such comic opera interchangeable names like Salarino, Solario and Salerio that they have often been lumped together as "the salads," or the "sallies"; as well there is the garrulous Gratiano, a court jester, who remains steadfastly loyal to Bassanio. Shylock's servant Launcelot Gobbo, a clown, and his addle- brained father, Old Gobbo, appear intermittently to perform a stand-up comedy routine. The younger Gobbo fills a minor go-between role in the growing rift between Shylock and his turncoat daughter Jessica, a self-hating Jewess, as she plans an elopement with the Christian Lorenzo.

Meanwhile the second major plot, the "casket-motive," intrudes as Portia (who lives not in urban Venice but in suburban Belmont, a kind of Renaissance "gated community") struggles with a bizarre edict from her late father, a control freak, that forbids her marriage to any man who chooses the wrong casket of gold, silver, or lead. That lure brings suitors to Belmont from the four corners of the earth, including England, Germany, and Morocco, all of whom come under the searching and pitiless eyes of Portia and her loyal waiting woman, Nerissa. As the archetypal rich girl in the suburbs, Portia is variously interpreted as a paragon of virtue, or again in contemporary deconstructive mode as a nasty little prig adept in manipulation and double-dealing. Her style, labeled by John Velz as the " Ovidian Grotesque," has been traced back to Ovid's Medea, who is an "innocent virgin...yet...a witch with supernal powers," [2] and who is mentioned in the play.

The stage is crowded with other characters, enough for a Gilbert and Sullivan comic operetta, that must have strained the resources of an Elizabethan acting company. They include Shylock's ubiquitous friend, Tubal, another Jewish moneylender; the lofty Duke of Venice who presides over the trial of Antonio; a jailer; and a galaxy of magnificoes, musicians, officers and attendants of the court. To sort out this rich assortment of humanity everything depends on the interaction of audience and actors, who may or may not see eye to eye on what Shakespeare would find acceptable. Little wonder that at times the play has been seen as "a tragedy," and again as a "comedy."

History of Performances on Stage

The play's long stage history reflects traces of these many points of view that usually coincide with the unconscious metaphysic of any epoch. As the Quarto title page advertises, it was "at divers times acted by the Lord Chamberlaine, his Seruants." [3] and twice at court in 1605 by the King's Men, [4] yet for arcane reasons the play did not appear on English public stages for several decades. A very early production was George Granville's 1701 free style adaptation, "The Jew of Venice," which included the famous Anne Bracegirdle as Portia, playwright Thomas Betterton as Bassanio, and Thomas Doggett as a miserly Shylock, though Granville's liberties with the text put it outside the main stream of *Merchant* productions. The stage life of Granville's production has been estimated at some forty years, but Charles Edelman, challenging this data as seriously exaggerated, sees Granville's play as not seriously influencing subsequent performance history.[5] Charles Macklin's 1741 production introduced its own innovations, with Macklin portraying a "sullen,

2   John W. Velz, "Portia and the Ovidian Grotesque," The Merchant of Venice: *New Critical Essays* eds. John Mahon and Ellen Mahon (New York: Routledge, 2002), p. 187..

3   E.K. Chambers, *William Shakespeare: A Study of Facts and Problems* I (Oxford : Clarendon Press, 1930), p. 368.

4   Bulman, p. 13.

5   *The Merchant of Venice*. Edited by Charles Edelman (Cambridge UP, 2002), p. 7.

malevolent Jew…terrifying the audience by his ferocity."[6] By 1814 Edmund Kean in contrast offered a "suffering" Shylock who was indeed "the tragedy of a man," [7] who had been subjected to unbearable abuse.

With nineteenth-century Victorian England emerging as a mercantile powerhouse, actor/managers like Henry Irving, Charles Macklin, Charles Kean, and William Charles Macready made the *Merchant* a mirror to contemporary society, where bourgeois mercantile values increasingly challenged the aristocratic values of the dominant land owning class. There was a struggle also to create a Shylock consistent, as Alexander Pope put it, with "the Jew that Shakespeare drew,"[8] Henry Irving introduced a Shylock modeled on the dignity of Levantine Jewry that he had witnessed in his travels. Ellen Terry's brilliant style with a hint of the "new woman" in her manner stimulated fresh curiosity about the enigmatic lady of Belmont, who by the mid-nineteenth century had been reinvented as a Victorian *grand dâme*. In 1851 Edmund Kean's gifted son, Charles, produced a *Merchant* of incomparable lavishness that delighted audiences already hypnotized by the popular image of a fairy-land Venice of arching bridges and quaint canals. Stage designers came under the influence of eighteenth-century romantic artists like Canaletto, whose image of the Grand Canal fueled British enthusiasm for the wonders of Venice. Mark Thornton Burnett has pointed out how the lavish Radford *Merchant* offers an "aestheticization of Venice" as a form of "anaesthetization," or "a means of offsetting what is unpalatable about the film's subject and its content."[9]

The resulting interpretations fall between views of the money-lender as a frightening monster in the style of Charles Macklin, and at the other extreme as a tormented creature whose response to injustice justifies his pathological hatred of Christians. Edmund Kean was one of the first to present a Shylock who was more sinned against than a sinner. Moreover, the nineteenth-century obsession with complicated, upholstered sets frequently forced drastic textual transpositions and deletions to make the action fit the scenery. In the *Merchant* the grandiose stage sets and choruses of Italian opera, which in turn had been influenced by Shakespeare, trickled into the *mise-en-scène*. The familiar tension between word and spectacle, which can be traced back to the quarrels between set designer Inigo Jones and poet Ben Jonson at the court of James the First, persisted in nineteenth-century theatre, but enthusiasm for stage spectacle edged out the word. The emerging technology of film at the close of the nineteenth century would soon intervene in this rivalry. One director, William Poel, sought to restore Shakespeare's plays to the "simplicity

---

6   *The Merchant of Venice*, Edited by M.M. Mahood (Cambridge UP, 2003), P. 43.

7   Toby Lelyveld, "Edmund Kean as Shylock," in *The Merchant of Venice. William Shakespeare*, edited by Leah S. Marcus (New York: W.W. Norton, 2006), p. 220.

8   Edelman, p. 8.

9   *Filming Shakespeare in the Global Marketplace* (London: Palgrave/Macmillan, 2007), p. 88.

and swiftness" of the Elizabethan stage,[10] though he was rowing upstream given the desire of the times for visual gratification.

The calamitous events of World War I, when millions lost their lives in a wasteland of folly, shattered all aspects of Victorian culture. By 1932 William Bridges-Adams, director of Stratford's Shakespeare Theatre, breaking with the conservative policies of neo-Victorian director William Benson, brought a leading Russian theatrical director, Theodore Komisarjevsky, to Stratford. Reflecting the vanguard of the twentieth-century artistic revolution, the immediate post-revolutionary phase of the Bolshevik revolution was steeped in Marxism and avant-garde art before its anarchistic tendencies were crushed by bureaucratic Stalinism. The Expressionistic and Surrealistic motifs of European art grabbed center stage in Komisarjevsky's *Merchant*, whose skewed bridges and tilted buildings replaced the conventional artistic views of a romantic Venice, much to the bafflement of many British conservatives. Moreover the impudent stage sets encouraged a carnivalesque spirit, so that even Shylock took on a clownish guise.

While Komisarjevsky's anarchistic style sometimes repelled as much as it attracted audiences, it did provide an opening wedge for bold dramaturgy. Directors no longer needed to think only about what the play meant to Shakespeare and his times but also what it could mean to twentieth-century audiences. The strict codes of Victorian protocols began to unravel and it became increasingly acceptable to reinvent the plays in a modern context, though conservatives never ceased denouncing such innovations as heretical. The 1970 Old Vic production directed by Jonathan Miller put Laurence Olivier's Shylock in a conservative Edwardian business suit that virtually took him by osmosis into the prevailing Venetian ethos, though the yarmulke under his hat certified to his Jewishness. Trevor Nunn's 1999 conception put the men in business suits and even moved the venue from Venice to the sleazy post-World War I "Cabaret" style Berlin cafes.

The whiff of a taboo homosexual relationship between Antonio and Bassanio has increasingly infiltrated productions, perhaps initially with a 1965 RSC presentation directed by Clifford Williams.[11] A hint of an erotic ardor between Antonio and Bassanio has since then become almost a stage clichè, though since it is often wrapped in secrecy it ends up with the same evasiveness of the "don't ask, don't tell" policy of the U.S. military. In the last several decades memorable productions by Michael Langham (1960), Orson Welles (unfinished, 1969), Terry Hands (1971), John Barton (1981), Peter Hall with Dustin Hoffman as Shylock (1989), and Peter Sellars (1994) have offered a plethora of directorial interpretations. A recent experiment was Don Selwyn's *Maori Merchant of Venice* (2002), produced in New Zealand as a merger of Shakespeare with aboriginal culture. With sub-titles in English, it tells of the Jewish money lender (Hairoka), and incorporates Maori

---

10   Jay L. Halio, ed. *The Merchant of Venice* (Oxford: The Clarendon Press, 1993), p.70.

11   Miriam Gilbert, *The Merchant of Venice* (Stratford Shakespeare Birthplace Trust: Arden, 2002), p.54.

art, music, and culture. The Prince of Morocco, for example, is welcomed with conch shell and *karanga* (a female cry of welcome). In New York City this year (2007) F. Murray Abraham did side-by-side performances as Barabas in Marlowe's *The Jew of Malta* and Shylock in *The Merchant of Venice*. He interpreted Shylock as even darker than Marlowe's notoriously wicked Barabas. The Abraham production carried recontextualization to the ultimate degree with a set showing "an internet café with cell phones, computers, blackberries, and, running across the top, stock market quotes." [12] The trend to modernizing costume and sets continues unabated despite howls from Shakespeare "purists." In 2007 Kenneth Branagh's televised *As You Like It* on HBO re-imagined the setting as Japanese, putting the actors into semi-Nipponese wardrobes, and turning Charles the wrestler into a plump Sumo contender. When successful, by putting the play into a fresh context these radical forays often open up otherwise unenvisaged insights.

History of Cinematic Adaptations

The pioneering late nineteenth-century moviemakers wasted little time in putting fragments of Shakespeare on celluloid, as novelties to be shown to the unwashed masses in music halls, fair grounds, and vaudeville houses. In 1900 the fabled Sarah Bernhardt brought glamour to déclassé movies by appearing on screen at the Paris Exhibition in her celebrated stage role as a cross-dressed Hamlet. In 1899 Sir Herbert Beerbohm Tree recorded segments of *King John* from the Her Majesty's Theatre production in London. In 1902 the French motion picture industry released *The Merchant of Venice, Une mesavanture de Shylock,* directed by pioneering Georges Méliès, though how closely this lost film adhered to Shakespeare's text and how much it simply usurped the title cannot be told. An Italian Film d'Arte version of *Merchant* starring Ermete Novelli and Francesca Bertini was one of the best of the silents, even though it skewed the drama around to focus so much on Lorenzo and Jessica that it could be legitimately retitled "Daughter of Shylock." The Italians were very good with Shakespeare's Mediterranean plays, often endowing them with a Verdiesque grandeur, and in this tinted film ample use was made of the quaint streets and canals of Venice. A plump Portia occupies a luxurious villa in Belmont, while Shylock in the Macklin tradition is cruel and obsessed, being quiveringly turned on by the act of whetting his knife at the beginning of the trial scene. In 1913 a French *Merchant* featured Harry Bauer as a greedy Shylock, who ironically a decade later was arrested and tortured by the Gestapo. A 1916 British version starring Matheson Lang as Shylock and Kathleen Jones as Jessica recruited a cast from London's St. James Theatre. Taking advantage of the tangled plots in the play, this version too concentrated on the troubled relationship between Jessica and Shylock.

The 1980 BBC production of *The Merchant of Venice* was a part of a Quixotic scheme to produce all of Shakespeare's plays for television as a kind of folio

---

12   Irene G. Dash, "The Theater for a New Audience's *Merchant of Venice* and *Jew of Malta," The Shakespeare Newsletter* (Winter 06/07), 103.

in moving images. Perhaps because of the heavy corporate funding there was a conservative bias from the start, with the producers following in the tradition of the suburban-oriented culture of the BBC Masterpiece Theatre, and adding to that the pedagogical flavor of the British "schools" plays, made for student consumption. In the "schools" plays it was important for Shakespeare to be "as written," and to avoid any stage business that might prove anathema to stuffy school trustees. So much, in other words, for any of the wild innovations of a Theodore Komisarjevsky.

The opening sequence of *Merchant* offers an index to the triumphs and defects of the entire project. Visually it continued the BBC policy of emulating the master artists of Shakespeare's own lifetime in designing the *mise en scène*. For Portia's Belmont the model could have been Titian; for Venice, Canaletto. Belmont swirls in a mist of gauzy color, and a recurring shot of a gazebo underscores its suburban preciousness. The timidity about enraging Bardolaters is readily apparent when a magnificently costumed John Franklyn-Robbins speaks of his depression in a delicate garden against a backdrop of soft pinks and pastels. The contrast between his morose feelings and his spritely surroundings leaves the spectator wondering if some part of the equation has been overlooked. Franklyn-Robbins does not act so much as he orates. For that matter, all the characters have a tendency to speechify, to pontificate, to sing as if in an opera rather than to dig deeply for the inner meaning. Too frequently they fail to listen or to look at one another. It is here that the presence of American actors, blissfully ignorant of Shakespearean elocution but fascinated by "method" acting in the style of Marlon Brando, might have helped. Comparison of Franklyn-Robbins' dandified Antonio with David Bamber's rumpled mediocrity in the Nunn *Merchant* suggests catastrophic miscasting by the BBC.

Having said all that, it is only fair to note that putting the melancholy Antonio in this idyllic surrounding might also underscore the way in which the action of the play itself is always threatened by dark forces, being in one plot a romance and in another a tragedy. If the director had placed a thunder cloud over the garden, the symbolism would have been perfect.

Happily, however, the BBC production also has fabulous moments, the most memorable being Warren Mitchell's portrayal of Shylock. Mitchell's unrelenting expenditure of energy undergoes a microanalysis on the small screen of television. Every nuance of expression from drooping eyes to quivering chin, every gesture of hand or arm, every wrinkle on the sagging face, merge to express his inner sorrow and rage. He does all of this, however, under control without resorting to the flagrant scenery chewing of lesser talents.

In 2002 Michael Radford's *The Merchant of Venice* exceeded all other filmic treatments by the color and pace in which it transferred verbal into rich but not quite gaudy visual images. A distinguished cast included not only Al Pacino (a.k.a. Michael Corleone) as Shylock but also Joseph Fiennes (of *Shakespeare in Love* fame) as Bassanio, and Jeremy Irons as Antonio. Bassanio and Antonio mime homosexual proclivities quite clearly (in one instance a full kiss on the mouth), which so many critics have taken as the source of Antonio's cryptic depression in the play's opening lines ("In sooth I know not why I am so sad. / It wearies me…"). Newcomer Lynn Collins makes a lovely and apparently uncomplicated Portia untouched by the Machiavellianism sometimes attributed to her by post-modernists, or the dual personality inspired by Ovid's Medea. The silent screen technique of an explanatory scroll narrates the cultural context of Jewish misery in 1596 Venetian ghettos.

The establishing shot of an extratextual street fight on the Rialto bridge is a *tour de force* that is supposed to include nearly all the film's cast, but beyond that it gives a snapshot of the tensions in contemporary Venice, and in a final flash of inspiration offers a dumb show for the play's major themes.. The ugly melee on the Rialto shows an innocent Jew in a ghetto-style red hat being tossed into the brackish canal by a mob of anti-Semites. A shaken Shylock, played by Al Pacino, is humiliated by Antonio who "spit[s] upon [his] Jewish gaberdine" (1.3.106), a cruelty reminiscent of Adolf Hitler's storm troopers, who enjoyed nothing more than bullying helpless Jews.

This montage of close shots steeped in post-Holocaust attitudes shifts from the wretched Jew being dumped into the canal to a cascade of blood gushing from the throat of a goat, dying and bleating with unspeakable fright. The shock image of the sacrificed goat becomes metonymy for the victimized Jew, or "scapegoat." The goat's blood foreshadows Shylock's comparison of the worth of a pound of "muttons, beefs, or goats"(1.3.160), as well as Portia's warning in the trial scene against Shylock's taking from Antonio "not a jot of blood"(4.1.302). At a market stall, an unpalatable chunk of raw goat meat, perhaps a pound in weight, is butchered for retail consumption, a clear portent to Antonio's own terrifying predicament. A nearby butcher's scale anticipates Shylock's morbid "balance" for the trial of Antonio. Wrapped in butcher's paper, the pound of goat flesh is carried off lovingly, even erotically, by Shylock, who before the Duke and all of Venice will soon himself serve as a scapegoat.

Radford's camera swallows up the fairy-land beauty of a Venice that has changed hardly at all in four centuries. The only difficulty is that digestion does not always follow the swallowing. The film is a riot of color showing the streets and canals, and the lavish costumes, designed to endow Venice with mystical charm. The arsenal of filters for bringing about these effects often creates a blur of color rather than pristine clarity. At Belmont Portia's very name suggests a portal open to others, though Grace Tiffany has shown how Portia's doorway is open only to the socially acceptable, Morocco and people of his "complexion" being ostracized. [13] Portia, in testing her suitors with the mystery of the caskets, enacts a social competition more terrifying in its ruthlessness than the commercial bargaining in Venice.

While long shots exploit the marvelous landmarks of the city—the Doge's Palace, the Grand Canal, St. Mark's Square, etc., Radford is also expert with the telling close shot when the "turquoise" ring that Leah had given Shylock when he was a bachelor surfaces in analytical shots. Here Radford fleshes out the Shakespeare

---

13   "Names in *The Merchant of Venice*," in Mahon, 361.

text that wins so much sympathy for a Shylock seen as victimized by a daughter who bargained away his ring for a monkey. Shylock cries out in anguish that he would not have "...given it for a wilderness of monkeys" (3.1.90). Radford intervenes with an extratexual shot of a carefree Jessica actually toying with the ring, though at the close of the film a newly chastened and distraught Jessica looks out to sea at a cluster of anglers shooting arrows at fish ("to bait fish withal"[3.1.39] her father had said). The turquoise ring remains fixed in close up on her finger. It is never explicit in Shakespeare's narrative that Jessica felt remorse for her wicked behavior, but it has been observed that the film "...functions to restore [Jessica's] imagined language and give voice to a past that is unspeakable."[14] If so, Radford has traveled deeply into his own imagination to supply subtext for what Shakespeare withheld. Shylock's (or Leah's) ring, of course, can also then be linked thematically to the wedding rings of Bassanio and Gratiano that lead to an ending with full opportunity for Portia's and Jessica's vituperative responses to an apparent betrayal. Jessica's melancholy at the end of the film, conveying a sense of the sadness of the human condition, curiously echoes Antonio's at the beginning of the play. "I am never merry when I hear sweet music" (5.1.69) says Jessica to Lorenzo in the lyrical fifth act, as if anxious to put a caption on her inner despair and the inner despair within the play.

Few productions of the *Merchant*, however, have come even close to Trevor Nunn's superb 2001 television version of a 1999 National Theatre production, which in its tightness and disciplined choreography approaches the precision of a great symphony orchestra. Talented cast members include Derbhle Crotty as an elegant but severe Portia, David Bamber as a pudgy and somewhat forlorn Antonio, and Henry Goodman as a Shylock with the capacity to be simultaneously menacing and vulnerable. Nunn did not hesitate to exploit the volatile feud between Shylock the lonely widower and his recalcitrant daughter, Jessica, a female "Jazz Singer" like the defiant cantor's son in Al Jolson's famous movie. In one nostalgic but extratextual scene the two sing a traditional Hebrew love duet, "Eshet Chayil," celebrating the virtues of a good housewife.[15] Then, in a sharply contrasting episode, Shylock screams at Jessica for not scrubbing hard enough on the pots and pans. In a really ugly moment he slaps her across the face. These rumblings signify the bright and dark moods of Shylock, and suggest the paralyzing emotional furor in the heart of Jessica, who is both consecrated to and yet alienated from her cantankerous father. The film comes very close to capturing the paradox at the core of the play, which is that the human condition forever struggles through a forest of sunshine and shadow, never quite winning nor quite losing.

Derbhle Crotty as Portia frosts her minimalist Belmont villa with an icy personality to ensure, unlike Jessica, that her deceased father's mandates prevail, though there are hints to the contrary. Her houseful of loyal and well-drilled

---

14   Mark Thornton Burnett, *Filming Shakespeare in the Global Marketplace* (New York and London: Palgrave, 2007), p.104.

15   Edelman, pp.265-6.

servant women, dressed in the matronly black-and-white uniforms of female prison attendants, are a further index into the inner psyche of this enigmatic woman. Few who see this production will forget the moment when Crotty kneels on a hassock with her back as stiff and erect as a guardsman, and crosses herself while Bassanio examines the caskets. After Bassanio makes the fateful choice of the lead casket, Nunn improvises from the subtext when he signals the manifest disappointment of a serving girl at the news that Gratiano will take Nerissa as a wife, a hint that perfectly fits the *Gestalt* of Gratiano's character as a roué who would revel in assignations with the downstairs help. Since Nunn actually employs only 29 per cent of the Quarto text, there is leisure for such whimsical cinematic additions.

A full theatrical history of the extraordinarily popular *The Merchant of Venice* requires many volumes. The brief sketch offered here, along with the books recommended in the bibliography, will provide a head start into a fascinating chapter of stage history.

THE MERCHANT OF VENICE

DRAMATIS PERSONAE

The Duke of Venice.
The Prince of Morocco,
The Prince of Arragon, } suitors to Portia.
Antonio, a Venetian merchant.
Bassanio, his friend, suitor to Portia.
Solanio,
Salerio, } friends to Antonio and Bassanio.
Gratiano,
Lorenzo, in love with Jessica.
Shylock, a Jew.
Tubal, a Jew, his friend.
Launcelot Gobbo, a clown, servant to Shylock.
Old Gobbo, father to Launcelot.
Leonardo, servant to Bassanio.
Balthasar, } servants to Portia.
Stephano,

Portia, an heiress.
Nerissa, her waiting gentlewoman.
Jessica, daughter to Shylock.

Magnificoes, Officers, Jailer, Servants, and other *Attendants.*

SCENE.—*Partly at Venice and partly at Belmont, Portia's estate.*

1

ACT I

SCENE I. [*Venice. A street.*]†

Enter Antonio, Salerio, *and* Solanio.

ANT.   In sooth, I know not why I am so sad.‡
It wearies me; you say it wearies you; *personification*
But how I caught it, found it, or came by it,
What stuff 'tis made of, whereof it is born,
I am to learn;   5
And such a want-wit sadness makes of me
That I have much ado to know myself.

SALER.   Your mind is tossing on the ocean;
There where your argosies with portly sail—
Like signiors and rich burghers on the flood,   10
Or, as it were, the pageants of the sea—
Do overpeer the petty traffickers,
That cursy to them, do them reverence,
As they fly by them with their woven wings.

ACT I. SCENE I.
1. **I know not why I am so sad.** Shakespeare was fond of "presentiments" (premonitions, or vague expectations), which might be seen here as evidence of melancholy, or in modern terms "depression." [K.R.].

---

†   In the BBC version, a somewhat aged Antonio played by John Franklyn-Robbins speaks his lines like a talking head against a bare backdrop that speaks of economy in the production. Most modern productions, as in the Nunn version, set this scene in a café, where a boozy and somewhat sinister atmosphere reflect the anxieties of the world of commerce and trade, gain and loss.

‡   Film and television directors have been impressively creative in discovering ways to open this play. Jack Gold (BBC 1980) costumed John Franklyn-Robbins (Antonio) as an Elizabethan courtier, who first appears alone on the screen, a "talking head." He then recites his melancholy lines to Salerio and Salanio in a formal "Shakespearian" style, against the backdrop of an idealized semi-pastoral stage. Antonio's stiffness sets the tone for the entire production, whose opening set favors uppity Belmont over grubby Venice. Trevor Nunn's TV movie (UK 2001) takes a bold new tack, as his Antonio (David Bamber), a tired entrepreneur in a twentieth-century business suit, tries hard to be entertained with his cronies in a sleazy Berlin cabaret in Weimar Germany (c.1922). In another approach, Michael Radford in his major film starring Al Pacino as Shylock exploits all the techniques of contemporary film editing. He employs an old-fashioned silent screen technique of a scroll to explain the full extent of Venetian anti-Semitism, which reflects the director's desire to set the film in its historical context. He freely creates an extra-textual world with a daring montage centered on Venice's famous Rialto bridge, which in an array of quick cuts and rapid editing foreshadows the film's major events. There is a glimpse of Antonio spitting on Shylock, a ghastly shot of a sacrificed goat from whose slit throat blood copiously gushes, a fanatical priest in a gondola haranguing citizens about the wickedness of the Jews. The goat's scapegoat status mirrors Shylock's fate. [K.R.]

Radford's (2002) commitment to embedding the play in its historical context is supported by the use of an old-fashioned silent film scroll informing the audience about Venetian antagonism to Jews, and a montage of anti-Semitic rioting on the Rialto bridge. In the turmoil this poor man is about to be tossed into the canal, and elsewhere is a glimpse of Antonio (Jeremy Irons) spitting on Shylock (Al Pacino).

SOLAN.   Believe me, sir, had I such venture forth,   15
            The better part of my affections would
            Be with my hopes abroad. I should be still
            Plucking the grass to know where sits the wind,
            Piring in maps for ports, and piers, and roads;
            And every object that might make me fear   20
            Misfortune to my ventures, out of doubt
            Would make me sad.

SALER.   My wind, cooling my broth,
            Would blow me to an ague when I thought
            What harm a wind too great might do at sea.
            I should not see the sandy hourglass run   25
            But I should think of shallows and of flats,
            And see my wealthy Andrew dock'd in sand,
            Vailing her high top lower than her ribs
            To kiss her burial. Should I go to church*
            And see the holy edifice of stone   30
            And not bethink me straight of dangerous rocks,

24. **an ague:** i.e., a fit of trembling fear. 26. **flats:** sand bars (apparently), or "mud flats" near the coast. 27. **Andrew.** The name of a ship originally, the captured Spanish St. Andrès, which apparently went aground in the shoals of the English channel, c.f. Mahood [K.R.].28. **Vailing:** lowering, declining.

*   Salerio's imaginative discovery of the residue of a shipwreck in every object around him makes a clinical study of obsessive psychology. [K.R.]

Which, touching but my gentle vessel's side,   *material goods →*
Would scatter all her spices on the stream,   *feminity → purity*
Enrobe the roaring waters with my silks,
And, in a word, but even now worth this,   35
And now worth nothing? Shall I have the thought
To think on this, and shall I lack the thought   *risk in venturing*
That such a thing bechanc'd would make me sad?   *into love*
But tell not me! I know Antonio
Is sad to think upon his merchandise.   40

ANT.   Believe me, no. I thank my fortune for it,
My ventures are not in one bottom trusted,
Nor to one place; nor is my whole estate
Upon the fortune of this present year.
Therefore my merchandise makes me not sad.   45

SOLAN.   Why, then you are in love.   *two emotions: sad + in love*

ANT.   Fie, fie!

SOLAN.   Not in love neither? Then let us say you are sad
Because you are not merry; and 'twere as easy
For you to laugh, and leap, and say you are merry
Because you are not sad. Now, by two-headed Janus,   50
Nature hath fram'd strange fellows in her time:
Some that will evermore peep through their eyes,
And laugh like parrots at a bagpiper;
And other of such vinegar aspect
That they'll not show their teeth in way of smile,   55
Though Nestor swear the jest be laughable.

                 Enter Bassanio, Lorenzo, *and* Gratiano.

Here comes Bassanio, your most noble kinsman,
Gratiano, and Lorenzo. Fare ye well.
We leave you now with better company.

SALER.   I would have stay'd till I had made you merry,   60
If worthier friends had not prevented me.

---

35. **but even now,** etc. The shorthand is obvious. In a word, "I should always be thinking 'At this moment I am worth so much, at the next moment worth nothing at all,'". 36. **thought:** power of thinking. Note Shakespeare's rhetorical habit of repeating the same word [K.R.] 38. **bechanc'd:** if it happened. 39. **But tell not me!** i.e., don't try to make me believe anything else—an expression of conviction. 42. **bottom:** ship. 50. **by two-headed Janus.** Janus, the Roman god of doors and entrances, was represented with two faces. 52. **peep through their eyes:** i.e., look with their eyes half-closed when they affect laughter. 54. **aspéct.** Accented on the second syllable. 56. **Nestor:** the old councillor of the Greeks in the Trojan War who had lived through three generations, cited as a grave and dignified person unlikely to laugh easily, or at any trivial or indifferent jest. [K.R.]. 61. **prevented:** intervened by coming too soon [K.R.].

ANT.   Your worth is very dear in my regard.
         I take it your own business calls on you,
         And you embrace th' occasion to depart.

SALER.   Good morrow, my good lords.   65

BASS.   Good signiors both, when shall we laugh? Say, when?
         You grow exceeding strange. Must it be so?

SALER.   We'll make our leisures to attend on yours.

                                    Exeunt Salerio and Solanio.

LOR.   My Lord Bassanio, since you have found Antonio,
         We two will leave you; but at dinner time   70
         I pray you have in mind where we must meet.

BASS.   I will not fail you.

GRA.   You look not well, Signior Antonio.
         You have too much respect upon the world;
         They lose it that do buy it with much care.   75
         Believe me, you are marvellously chang'd.

ANT.   I hold the world but as the world, Gratiano—
         A stage, where every man must play a part, *acknowledgement
         And mine a sad one.   of the act of a play*

GRA.   Let me play the fool. *acting as a character
         With mirth and laughter let old wrinkles come, within character*   80
         And let my liver rather heat with wine
         Than my heart cool with mortifying groans.
         Why should a man whose blood is warm within
         Sit like his grandsire cut in alablaster?
         Sleep when he wakes? and creep into the jaundice   85
         By being peevish? I tell thee what, Antonio—

---

62. **Your worth,** etc.: highly valued by me [K.R.]. 64. **occasion:** opportunity. 65. **Good morrow:** good morning. The proper salutation until noon, after which "good even" was used. 66. **when shall we laugh?** when shall we have a relaxed meeting? [K.R.]. 67. **You grow exceeding strange:** We see very little of each other nowadays. 68. **We'll make our leisures to attend on yours:** i.e., we will try to make our free time coincide with yours in order to meet you and enjoy your company [K.R.]. 74. **respect upon the world:** regard for worldly affairs or prosperity. 75. **They lose it,** etc.: People trapped in the "rat race" for success may die in the effort [K.R.]. Cf. the Biblical "Whosoever will save his life shall lose it." 78. **A stage.** "All the world's a stage" was a common saying in Elizabethan times, its most famous example being in *As You Like It* (2.7). Antonio's response draws on this same figure [K.R.]. "I account this world a tedious Theatre / For I doe play a part in't." 79. Gratiano does literally "play the fool" in the opinion of other characters in the play [K.R.]. 80. **old wrinkles:** the wrinkles of old age. 81. **let my liver rather heat.** Drinking allegedly heated the liver. 82. **mortifying:** deadening, reducing the vitality. Every sigh was supposed to draw a drop of blood from the heart. 84. **alablaster.** A form of gypsum often used by sculptors [K.R.]. 85. **Sleep when he wakes?** So slothful even in his waking hours that he may be said to be asleep?—**creep into the jaundice.** The verb *creep* suggests that a contributory cause of the jaundice would be his sluggishness and inactivity. 86. **peevish.** Either "fretful" or "silly."

I love thee, and it is my love that speaks—
There are a sort of men whose visages
Do cream and mantle like a standing pond,
And do a wilful stillness entertain   90
With purpose to be dress'd in an opinion
Of wisdom, gravity, profound conceit;
As who should say, "I am Sir Oracle,
And when I ope my lips, let no dog bark!"
O my Antonio, I do know of these   95
That therefore only are reputed wise
For saying nothing; when, I am very sure,
If they should speak, would almost damn those ears
Which, hearing them, would call their brothers fools.
I'll tell thee more of this another time.   100
But fish not with this melancholy bait
For this fool gudgeon, this opinion.
Come, good Lorenzo. Fare ye well awhile.
I'll end my exhortation after dinner.

LOR.   Well, we will leave you then till dinner time.   105
I must be one of these same dumb wise men,
For Gratiano never lets me speak.

GRA.   Well, keep me company but two years moe,
Thou shalt not know the sound of thine own tongue.

ANT.   Fare you well. I'll grow a talker for this gear.   110

GRA.   Thanks, i' faith; for silence is only commendable
In a neat's tongue dried and a maid not vendible.

                                    Exeunt [*Gratiano and Lorenzo*].

ANT.   Is that anything now?

---

89. **cream and mantle:** become covered with a mantle of scum— the sallow coating of melancholy which overspreads the face of a man in depression [K.R.].**standing:** stagnant. 90. **do.** The subject is *who,* to be supplied from "whose" in l. 88.—**stillness:** quietness of demeanour.—**entertain:** fake, assume. 91. **to be dress'd in an opinion:** to be clothed in a reputation. 92. **profound conceit:** profound power of thought. 93. **Sir Oracle.** Cf. Heywood, *A Challenge for Beauty* (ed. Pearson, V, 39): "Oh, master Oracle." 95. **I do know of these:** I know some of these, I know some such persons. 96. **only.** Emphatic. 98. **would.** The subject is "they," supplied from the preceding clause. 98. **would almost damn those ears,** etc. The harmful words would cause them to stop their ears 99. **would call their brothers fools.** This passage privileges the reading "damn" in the preceding line. The idea is that the hearers would call the speakers fools, and since the speakers are their brothers, this remark would bring down condemnation upon them 101-02. **fish not,** etc. To cheer him up, the garrulous Gratiano begs Antonio not to assume a melancholy demeanor with the purpose of getting a reputation for wisdom. He calls public opinion a fool gudgeon, a proverbially stupid fish easily caught. 108. **moe:** more. 110. **I'll grow a talker for this gear.** Said jestingly. *Gear* means "stuff" and here refers to Gratiano's idle chatter. Antonio replies, "your example has convinced me to become garrulous ("a chatterbox") too so that people will not think my silence is merely a subterfuge to make them think I am wise" [K.R.]. 112 **neat's tongue:** cow [K.R.]. 112. **vendible:** salable; i.e., of course, marriageable.

BASS.   Gratiano speaks an infinite deal of nothing, more than any man in
all Venice. His reasons are as two grains of wheat hid in two bushels
of chaff. You shall seek all day ere you find them; and when you have
them, they are not worth the search.   117

ANT.   Well, tell me now, what lady is the same
To whom you swore a secret pilgrimage
That you to-day promis'd to tell me of?   120

BASS.   'Tis not unknown to you, Antonio,
How much I have disabled mine estate
By something showing a more swelling port
Than my faint means would grant continuance;
Nor do I now make moan to be abridg'd   125
From such a noble rate; but my chief care
Is to come fairly off from the great debts
Wherein my time, something too prodigal,
Hath left me gag'd. To you, Antonio,
I owe the most, in money and in love;   *money + love
are coupled*   130
And from your love I have a warranty
To unburden all my plots and purposes
How to get clear of all the debts I owe.

ANT.   I pray you, good Bassanio, let me know it;
And if it stand, as you yourself still do,   135
Within the eye of honor, be assur'd
My purse, my person, my extremest means
Lie all unlock'd to your occasions.

BASS.   In my schooldays, when I had lost one shaft,
I shot his fellow of the selfsame flight   140
The selfsame way with more advised watch,
To find the other forth; and by adventuring both
I oft found both. I urge this childhood proof
Because what follows is pure innocence.

---

122. **disabled mine estate:** frittered away my assets [K.R.]. 123. **something:** somewhat—adverbial.—**a
more swelling port:** an extravagant life style 124. **faint means:** few assets **would grant continuance:**
would enable me to continue in. 125. **to be abridg'd:** falling into financial disaster 126. **rate:** style of
living. 128. **time:** life.—**prodigal:** wasteful 129. **gag'd:** pledged, entangled, engaged. 135-36. **if it
stand...Within the eye of honor:** if it fits accepted standards of honor [K.R.]. 138. **Occasions:** needs;
or, uses. 139. **when I had lost one shaft.** Shot an arrow into an unmowed field 140. **his fellow of the
selfsame flight:** another arrow of the same size and identically feathered, so that it was calculated to
fly exactly as far. *His,* of course, means "its." 142-43. **To find the other forth:** to find it out, to recover
it from its hiding place.—**this childhood proof:** this experience from the time of my childhood. 144.
pure innocence. The suggestion is that what follows, though it may sound childish, is, at all events,
meant as sincerely as it would be meant by a child. The proposition of Bassanio, whatever may be
thought of it, is, he says, undertaken with as sincere a hope of success and with as little guile as the trick
of shooting one arrow after another.

I owe you much, and, like a wilful youth, 145
That which I owe is lost; but if you please
To shoot another arrow that self way
Which you did shoot the first, I do not doubt,
As I will watch the aim, or to find both,
Or bring your latter hazard back again 150
And thankfully rest debtor for the first.

ANT. You know me well, and herein spend but time
To wind about my love with circumstance;
And out of doubt you do me now more wrong
In making question of my uttermost 155
Than if you had made waste of all I have.
Then do but say to me what I should do
That in your knowledge may by me be done,
And I am prest unto it. Therefore speak.

BASS. In Belmont is a lady richly left; _wants to downplay reason_ 160
And she is fair, and, fairer than that word, _of love_
Of wondrous virtues. Sometimes from her eyes
I did receive fair speechless messages.
Her name is Portia—nothing undervalu'd
To Cato's daughter, Brutus' Portia. 165
Nor is the wide world ignorant of her worth;
For the four winds blow in from every coast
Renowned suitors, and her sunny locks
Hang on her temples like a golden fleece,
Which makes her seat of Belmont Colchos' strond, 170
And many Jasons come in quest of her.
O my Antonio, had I but the means

---

145. **like a wilful youth:** as is the case with an extravagant young man's debts; or, perhaps, "and what I have borrowed of you I no longer possess, for I have spent it as a willful [careless] youth spends." 147. **that self way:** that selfsame way. 149. **As I will watch the aim:** watching the aim as sharply as I shall. Note that _as_ does not mean "since."—**or:** either. 151. **rest debtor:** remain your debtor. Bassanio means of course that he does not expect to lose what Antonio shall now lend him, at all events, even if he does not recover the former loss. 153. **To wind about my love with circumstance:** When making a request from someone who loves you there is no need to wrap your words in language (circumstance).154. **out of doubt:** beyond question. 155. **making question of my uttermost:** doubting that I will do my utmost to serve you. 159. **prest:** ready.. 160. **richly left:** left rich (by her father at his death). An excellent example of the common use of the adverb in -_ly_ to indicate condition, like an adjective. 161. **fairer than that word:** fairer than fairness itself; or, rather, "fairer than any words can describe." 162. **virtues:** excellent qualities of every kind, including accomplishments. The word was not restricted to moral qualities in Shakespeare's time.—**Sometimes from her eyes,** etc. This passage indicates clearly that Bassanio is in love, or thinks he is in love, with Portia. Whatever his motives, the entire passage is a profound rhapsody on romantic love. 164. **nothing undervalu'd To:** not at all less valuable than. 165. **Cato's daughter.** Cf. Portia in _Julius Cæsar_, 2.1. 170. **seat:** residence. Belmont is the name of Portia's estate.—**Colchos' strond:** strand, the shore of Colchis, the country of the Golden Fleece. Bassanio uses the _o_-form here with poetical intent.

To hold a rival place with one of them,
I have a mind presages me such thrift   *emphasis on financial gain*
That I should questionless be fortunate!   *double meaning*   175

ANT.   Thou know'st that all my fortunes are at sea;
Neither have I money, nor commodity
To raise a present sum. Therefore go forth;
Try what my credit can in Venice do.†
That shall be rack'd, even to the uttermost,   180
To furnish thee to Belmont to fair Portia.
Go presently enquire, and so will I,
Where money is; and I no question make
To have it of my trust, or for my sake.   *Exeunt*

SCENE II. [*Belmont. Portia's house.*]

prejudiced I against foreign

Enter Portia *with her waiting woman,* Nerissa‡

reflection of antonios first line

POR. *figure* By my troth, Nerissa, my little body is aweary of this great world. *both yearning*

NER. You would be, sweet madam, if your miseries were in the same
abundance as your good fortunes are; and yet, for aught I see, they are
as sick that surfeit with too much as they that starve with nothing. It
is no mean happiness, therefore, to be seated in the mean. Superfluity   *idea that acting a certain way ages you faster*
comes sooner by white hairs, but competency lives longer.   6

174. **a mind presages:** a mind which[presages] "anticipates"—with the common omission of the
relative pronoun..—**thrift:** thriving, success, fortune. 177. **commodity:** merchandise. 180. **rack'd:**
stretched (as the victim was tortured upon the rack, an instrument for inflicting unbearable agony by
stretching the body until the joints gave way). 182. **presently:** instantly. 184. **of my trust, or for my
sake:** on account of the confidence people have in me or else for the sake of friendship.
SCENE II.
1. **my little body is aweary of this great world.** Portia's parallel expression of melancholy echoes
Antonio's (1.1). at the opening of the first scene. 5. **in the mean:** the golden mean, to have neither too
much nor too little, with a quibble on "mean happiness." 5-6. **Superfluity comes sooner by white hairs:**
excessive riches get white hairs sooner.—**competency:** sufficiency of means for life's necessities [K.R.].

or has affect on your physical appearance

†   The successful attempt by Bassanio to persuade Antonio to finance the wooing of Portia is handled
sensitively in the BBC version, though the whole production suffers from an inability of the actors
to conceal the fact that they are acting. While Bassanio is talking about his love for Portia, who
is "richly left," Antonio remains frozen in the foreground to allow the audience to see how he
is struggling to control his emotions. He is after all being asked to bankroll his own emotional
demise. Eventually Antonio surrenders to the inevitable by agreeing to help Bassanio. The two men,
Antonio clearly the elder, embrace and part with words of endearment. Their underlying emotions
are tactfully suppressed but the acting makes plain that the true aggressive lover could be Antonio,
not Bassanio The erotic possibilities in the relationship remain buried in the subtext. [K.R.]

‡   Nerissa's social status is far beyond that of an upstairs maid, An intimate friend and confidante
of Portia, she comes from a good Venetian family. In the BBC version, the grand décor of Portia's
villa reinforces the sense of her as a very rich lady accustomed to owning the world. [K.R.]

POR.   Good sentences, and well pronounc'd.

NER.   They would be better if well followed.

POR.   If to do were as easy as to know what were good to do, chapels had
been churches, and poor men's cottages princes' palaces. It is a good
divine that follows his own instructions. I can easier teach twenty what
were good to be done than be one of the twenty to follow mine own
teaching. The brain may devise laws for the blood, but a hot temper
leaps o'er a cold decree: such a hare is madness the youth, to skip o'er
the meshes of good counsel the cripple. But this reasoning is not in
the fashion to choose me a husband. O me, the word "choose"! I may
neither choose who I would nor refuse who I dislike, so is the will of
a living daughter curb'd by the will of a dead father. Is it not hard,
Nerissa, that I cannot choose one nor refuse none?   19

NER.   Your father was ever virtuous; and holy men at their death have good
inspirations. Therefore the lott'ry that he hath devised in these three
chests of gold, silver, and lead, whereof who chooses his meaning
chooses you, will no doubt never be chosen by any rightly but one
who you shall rightly love. But what warmth is there in your affection
towards any of these princely suitors that are already come?   25

POR.   I pray thee overname them; and as thou namest them, I will describe
them; and according to my description level at my affection.†

---

7. **Good sentences:** good sententious remarks, good maxims. 9-10. **chapels had been churches:**
every poor little chapel in the world would have been enlarged into a church to hold the worshippers
clamoring to be let in.—**poor men's cottages,** etc.: many a poor man might have become a prince, since
a poor man's innate wisdom may be superior to any prince's actions. 13-15. **the blood:** the impulses and
passions.—**temper:** temperament.—**cold:** calm and considerate.—**to skip o'er the meshes:** i.e., the
meshes of the net [for catching hares] by means of which good counsel would restrain him. 16. **is not
in the fashion to choose me a husband:** but this reasoning cannot help me in choosing a husband. 17.
who I would. Though the reference is here general, yet it [perhaps] points back to Bassanio's confession
that Portia's eyes have sent him "fair speechless messages" (Bassanio's confession in 1.1.162-63). 18.
will of a dead father: testament. 19. **choose one nor refuse none:** i.e., cannot make up my mind at
the outset whom I love and choose him, but must allow every comer a trial at the lottery and accept the
winner, regardless of my own feelings. 20-25. Nerissa's enthusiastic advocacy of the motives of Portia's
father in setting up this arbitrary test seem designed to reassure the audience of his good intentions
[K.R.]. 22-23. **in these three chests:** in the form of these three chests, which constitute the lottery.—
whereof who chooses his meaning chooses you: the one who selects that one of them which your
father means to have selected (i.e., the one which, according to his intended symbolism, is the best of the
three gets you). 23-24. **one who you shall rightly love:** one who shall love you as you ought to be loved.
This optimism on Nerissa's part [continues to give] the impression that Bassanio is really in love with
Portia and not merely with her estate. 27. **affection:** feelings.—**level at my affection:** guess at the way
in which I feel toward them. *Level* means to "aim," and *aim* was often used as a synonym for *guess.*

---

†   In the Nunn version, Nerissa displays moving images of the suitors with a 16mm projector, a
gambit that adds a kind of modern Powerpoint element to the lengthy descriptons. [K.R.]

Portia (Derbhle Crotty), a lady "richly left," and Nerissa (Alex Kelly), her lady-in-waiting, discuss the shortcomings of Portia's would-be suitors with the help of a 16mm projector. (Nunn, 2001)

NER.   First, there is the Neapolitan prince.

POR.   Ay, that's a colt indeed, for he doth nothing but talk of his horse; and he makes it a great appropriation to his own good parts that he can shoe him himself. I am much afeard my lady his mother play'd false with a smith.   bastard   32

NER.   Then is there the County Palatine.

POR.   He doth nothing but frown; as who should say, "An you will not have me, choose!" He hears merry tales and smiles not. I fear he will prove the weeping philosopher when he grows old, being so full of unmannerly sadness in his youth. I had rather be married to a death's-head with a bone in his mouth than to either of these. God defend me from these two!

---

28. **the Neapolitan prince.** In the descriptions that follow, the supposed foibles of noblemen and gentlemen in the several nations referred to are hit off. Each suitor is made a type of his nation, according to the Elizabethan idea. Thus these passages, though they appear as the descriptions of particular men, resemble rather closely the Characters which were popular in the sixteenth century. 29. **a colt:** a frisky fellow. 30. **he makes it a great appropriation to his own good parts:** he regards it as something which adds much to his own accomplishments. *Appropriation* means literally "attribution." 33. **County:** count. 34-35. **An you will not have me, choose.** *Me* is of course emphatic. "If *I* do not satisfy you, choose," i.e., I should like to see who there is that you can possibly prefer to me. 36. **the weeping philosopher.** An allusion to Heraclitus.

NER.   How say you by the French lord, Monsieur Le Bon?   40

POR.   God made him, and therefore let him pass for a man. In truth, I
know it is a sin to be a mocker; but he—why, he hath a horse better
than the Neapolitan's, a better bad habit of frowning than the Count
Palatine. He is every man in no man. If a throstle sing, he falls straight
a-cap'ring; he will fence with his own shadow. If I should marry him,
I should marry twenty husbands. If he would despise me, I would
forgive him; for if he love me to madness, I shall never requite him.

NER.   What say you then to Falconbridge, the young baron of England?   48

POR.   You know I say nothing to him; for he understands not me, nor I him.
He hath neither Latin, French, nor Italian; and you will come into
the court and swear that I have a poor pennyworth in the English. He
is a proper man's picture; but alas! who can converse with a dumb-
show? How oddly he is suited! I think he bought his doublet in Italy,
his round hose in France, his bonnet in Germany, and his behaviour
everywhere.   55

NER.   What think you of the Scottish lord, his neighbour?

POR.   That he hath a neighbourly charity in him; for he borrowed a box of
the ear of the Englishman, and swore he would pay him again when he
was able. I think the Frenchman became his surety and seal'd under for
another.   60

NER.   How like you the young German, the Duke of Saxony's nephew?

POR.   Very vilely in the morning, when he is sober, and most vilely in the
afternoon, when he is drunk. When he is best, he is a little worse than
a man; and when he is worst, he is little better than a beast. An the
worst fall that ever fell, I hope I shall make shift to go without him.

NER.   If he should offer to choose, and choose the right casket, you should
refuse to perform your father's will if you should refuse to accept him.

---

46. **twenty husbands.** Because the Frenchman is so volatile; as Portia says, "He is every man in no
man." 50. **He hath neither Latin,** etc. The reluctance of the English to learn any foreign language
fluently was and is proverbial. Latin, used for purposes of diplomacy and international conversation,
was almost a living language among the educated. 51. **a poor pennyworth:** a small lot, i.e., a very slight
knowledge. 52-53. **proper:** handsome.—**dumb-show:** pantomime. Cf. the dumb show in *Hamlet.*—
suited: dressed.—**his doublet in Italy,** etc. The English gentleman's habit of ripping off the fashion
of every country was often satirized. [K.R.] 54. **his behavior everywhere.** Young English gentlemen
were specially prone to affect foreign manners. 56. The poverty of the Scots is here satirized. As to their
alleged willingness to accept an injury, this is a mere piece of playing to the gallery on Shakespeare's
part. The Scots were not popular, but they were well known as hot blooded antagonists. 59-60. **seal'd
under for another:** put his seal under the Scot's seal on a bond promising to pay. The suggestion is
that the Frenchman also received a box on the ear from the Englishman. 63. **when he is drunk.** The
drinking habits of the Danes and the Germans were notorious in Elizabethan times. 65. **fall:** happen.—
make shift: contrive. 66-67. Nerissa makes plain how Portia's father by his decree has entrapped Portia
[K.R.].—**you should refuse:** you certainly would refuse.

POR.	Therefore, for fear of the worst, I pray thee set a deep glass of Rhenish wine on the contrary casket; for, if the devil be within and that temptation without, I know he will choose it. I will do anything, Nerissa, ere I will be married to a sponge. 71
NER.	You need not fear, lady, the having any of these lords. They have acquainted me with their determinations; which is indeed to return to their home, and to trouble you with no more suit, unless you may be won by some other sort than your father's imposition, depending on the caskets. 76
POR.	If I live to be as old as Sibylla, I will die as chaste as Diana unless I be obtained by the manner of my father's will. I am glad this parcel of wooers are so reasonable, for there is not one among them but I dote on his very absence; and I pray God grant them a fair departure. 80
NER.	Do you not remember, lady, in your father's time, a Venetian, a scholar and a soldier, that came hither in company of the Marquis of Montferrat?
POR.	Yes, yes, it was Bassanio. As I think, so was he call'd. 84
NER.	True, madam. He, of all the men that ever my foolish eyes look'd upon, was the best deserving a fair lady.
POR.	I remember him well, and I remember him worthy of thy praise.

Enter a Servingman.

	How now? What news? 88
SERV.	The four strangers seek for you, madam, to take their leave; and there is a forerunner come from a fifth, the Prince of Morocco, who brings word the Prince his master will be here tonight. 91
POR.	If I could bid the fifth welcome with so good heart as I can bid the other four farewell, I should be glad of his approach. If he have the condition of a saint and the complexion of a devil, I had rather he should shrive me than wive me. 95

---

75. **by some other sort:** in some other manner.—**than your father's imposition:** than that imposed by your father. Possibly *sort* means "lot" in this line, but it is easier to take it in the sense of "manner." Cf. l. 78 below. By this device of making the suitors just described return without taking their luck with the caskets, Shakespeare affords additional variety. Several suitors are described in a lively fashion, but those who actually come to the test are an entirely different set. See 2.7. Of course all this serves to emphasize the truth of what Bassanio says in 1.1 167 ff.: "For the four winds blow in from every coast / Renowned suitors." 81. **Do you not remember, lady?** Nerissa, in her character of intimate lady-in-waiting and confidante, brings the question of Portia's relationship with Bassanio out into the open. Her question is designed to test the accuracy of her impression that Portia loves Bassanio. Any doubts in the minds of the audience are thus dispelled.[K.R.]—**in your father's time.** There is a subtle suggestion that Portia's father had not only known Bassanio but liked him. Perhaps he understood that Bassanio was exactly the kind of intelligent young man who would see through the deception of making the winning casket the outwardly least desirable. [K.R.]. 94. **condition:** character. 95. **shrive:** hear my confession, like a priest [K.R.].

Come, Nerissa. Sirrah, go before.
Whiles we shut the gate upon one wooer, another knocks at the door.

Exeunt.

SCENE III. [Venice. A public place.]

Enter Bassanio *with* Shylock *the Jew.*[†]

SHY.	Three thousand ducats—well.	
BASS.	Ay, sir, for three months.	
SHY.	For three months—well.	
BASS.	For the which, as I told you, Antonio shall be bound.	
SHY.	Antonio shall become bound—well.	5
BASS.	May you stead me? Will you pleasure me? Shall I know your answer?	
SHY.	Three thousand ducats for three months, and Antonio bound.	
BASS.	Your answer to that.	
SHY.	Antonio is a good man.	
BASS.	Have you heard any imputation to the contrary?	10
SHY.	Ho, no, no, no, no! My meaning in saying he is a good man is to have you understand me that he is sufficient. Yet his means are in supposition. He hath an argosy bound to Tripolis, another to the Indies. I understand, moreover, upon the Rialto, he hath a third at Mexico, a fourth for England, and other ventures he hath, squand'red abroad. But ships are but boards, sailors but men; there be land rats and water rats, land thieves and water thieves—I mean pirates;	

---

97. **Whiles:** while.
SCENE III.
1. The ducat was originally minted as a gold or silver coin in Venice but it gradually spread all over Europe as a standard legal tender. Its exact value in today's exchange is difficult to estimate. [K.R.]
5. **bound:** Antonio is legally committed to his contract. 6. **stead me:** accommodate me. 11. **good:** a good man—in the mercantile sense, "a solvent man." Bassanio apparently detects a tinge of doubt at this remark, as if Shylock had implied some defect in Antonio's character. 13. **supposition:** doubt—**argosy:** a great merchant ship. 14. **the Rialto:** the famous bridge in Venice which, with the street in the neighborhood, is the Venetian Exchange. 15. **squand'red:** scattered.

[†] This first glimpse of Shylock on stage already hints at his dual traits of villain and victim. Laurence Olivier appears as a thoroughly assimilated Jew in the Edwardian (c. 1880) period, whose manner and dress qualify him for acceptance in polite Venetian society. Jack Gold's Shylock, as played by Warren Mitchell, on the other hand, glories in playing up Shylock's stereotypical speech mannerisms and body language to accentuate his "Jewishness." Trevor Nunn's money lender (Henry Goodman) follows a middle ground in which, without either groveling or condescending to Christians, he nevertheless maintains an innate and powerful dignity. [K.R.]

and then there is the peril of waters, winds, and rocks. The man is, notwithstanding, sufficient. Three thousand ducats. I think I may take his bond.   20

BASS.   Be assur'd you may.

SHY.   I will be assur'd I may; and, that I may be assured, I will bethink me. May I speak with Antonio?

BASS.   If it please you to dine with us.   24

SHY.   Yes, to smell pork, to eat of the habitation which your prophet the Nazarite conjured the devil into! I will buy with you, sell with you, talk with you, walk with you, and so following; but I will not eat with you, drink with you, nor pray with you. What news on the Rialto? Who is he comes here?   29

Enter Antonio.

BASS.   This is Signior Antonio.

SHY.   [*aside*] How like a fawning publican he looks!‡
I hate him for he is a Christian;
But more for that in low simplicity
He lends out money gratis and brings down
The rate of usance here with us in Venice.   35
If I can catch him once upon the hip,
I will feed fat the ancient grudge I bear him.
He hates our sacred nation, and he rails,
Even there where merchants most do congregate,
On me, my bargains, and my well-won thrift,   40
Which he calls interest. Cursed be my tribe
If I forgive him!

BASS.   Shylock, do you hear?

SHY.   I am debating of my present store,
And by the near guess of my memory
I cannot instantly raise up the gross   45
Of full three thousand ducats. What of that?
Tubal, a wealthy Hebrew of my tribe,

---

22. **will.** Emphatic. 26. **your prophet the Nazarite.** The reference is to the miracle by which the evil spirits were sent into the herd of swine. 31. **publican**: A Jewish tax collector for the ancient Romans. 32. **for**: because. 35. **usance**: usury, i.e., interest. 36. **upon the hip.** A wrestling term, "in such a position that the wrestler, using his hip as a fulcrum, can throw his opponent." 40. **thrift**: thriving, prosperity—hence, property.

---

‡   Shylock's reputation for savagery originates in scenes like this one where he is in a vicious mood; elsewhere he may appear more a victim than a villain. [K.R.]

Will furnish me. But soft! How many months
Do you desire?—[*To Antonio*] Rest you fair, good signior!
Your worship was the last man in our mouths.   50

ANT.   Shylock, albeit I neither lend nor borrow
By taking nor by giving of excess,
Yet, to supply the ripe wants of my friend,
I'll break a custom. [*To Bassanio*] Is he yet possess'd
How much ye would?

SHY.   Ay, ay, three thousand ducats.   55

ANT.   And for three months.

SHY.   I had forgot—three months, you told me so.
Well then, your bond. And let me see—but hear you:
Methoughts you said you neither lend nor borrow
Upon advantage.

ANT.   I do never use it.   60

SHY.   When Jacob graz'd his uncle Laban's sheep—
This Jacob from our holy Abram was
(As his wise mother wrought in his behalf)
The third possessor; ay, he was the third—

ANT.   And what of him? Did he take interest?   65

SHY.   No, not take interest; not, as you would say,
Directly int'rest. Mark what Jacob did.
When Laban and himself were compremis'd
That all the eanlings which were streak'd and pied
Should fall as Jacob's hire, the ewes, being rank,   70
In end of autumn turned to the rams;
And when the work of generation was
Between these woolly breeders in the act,
The skilful shepherd pill'd me certain wands,
And, in the doing of the deed of kind,   75
He stuck them up before the fulsome ewes,
Who then conceiving, did in eaning time

49. **Rest you fair:** Shylock pretends to catch sight of Antonio at this moment. In *rest you fair, rest* means "may you remain," "may you be"; and so the expression is equivalent to "may you be well and prosperous." Cf Commonly distorted in the well-known Christmas Carol "God rest you, merry gentlemen," which is a misunderstanding for "God rest you merry, gentlemen." 52. **excess:** something over and above the principal—hence, "interest." 54. **possess'd:** informed. 60. **Upon advantage:** for interest. 61. **When Jacob graz'd,** etc. Shylock finds it impossible to refrain from defending the principle of taking interest by an example from the Bible. 63. **As his wise mother,** etc.: owing to the efforts which his wise mother made in his behalf. 68. **were compremis'd:** had made an agreement. 69. **eanlings:** yeanlings, i.e., lambs.—**pied:** variegated. 70. **rank:** in heat. 74. **pill'd:** stripped off.—**me.** ethical dative, i.e., "stripped off for me" [K.R.]. 75. **kind:** nature.

Fall parti-colour'd lambs, and those were Jacob's.
This was a way to thrive, and he was blest;
And thrift is blessing, if men steal it not.   80

ANT.   This was a venture, sir, that Jacob serv'd for;
A thing not in his power to bring to pass,
But sway'd and fashion'd by the hand of heaven.
Was this inserted to make interest good?
Or is your gold and silver ewes and rams?   85

SHY.   I cannot tell; I make it breed as fast. *breeding money w/ money*
But note me, signior.

ANT.   [*aside*] Mark you this, Bassanio,
The devil can cite Scripture for his purpose.
An evil soul, producing holy witness,
Is like a villain with a smiling cheek,   90
A goodly apple rotten at the heart.
O, what a goodly outside falsehood hath!

SHY.   Three thousand ducats—'tis a good round sum.
Three months from twelve—then, let me see, the rate—

ANT.   Well, Shylock, shall we be beholding to you?   95

SHY.   Signior Antonio, many a time and oft
In the Rialto you have rated me
About my moneys and my usances.
Still have I borne it with a patient shrug;
For suff'rance is the badge of all our tribe.   100
You call me misbeliever, cutthroat dog,
And spet upon my Jewish gaberdine,
And all for use of that which is mine own.
Well then, it now appears you need my help.
Go to then, you come to me and you say,   105
"Shylock, we would have moneys." You say so—

---

78. **Fall:** let fall. 81. **a venture.** Without denying the morality of Jacob's trick, Antonio holds that it was a fairly routine commercial venture. 84. **inserted:** i.e., in the Bible. 86. **I make it breed as fast.** The Greek word for "interest on money" is *tokos*, which also means "offspring." Aristotle argues that interest is wrong because it is unnatural that gold and silver should breed or have offspring, an argument similar to Antonio's at 1.3.124. 90. **a villain with a smiling cheek.** Cf. *Hamlet*, (1.5). "O villain, villain, smiling, damned villain." 92. **outside.** Accented on the first syllable. 97. **rated:** berated, scolded. [note the quibble on "rated" at line 99 where Shylock implies his resentment at the way that Antonio has evaluated ("rated") him [K.R.]]. **usances:** interest, usury. 100. **suff'rance:** patient endurance.—**the badge of all our tribe.** Shylock's bitterness grows out of a context in which throughout Europe at various times and places, the Jews were mandated to wear humiliating costumes or labels, a fact that gives peculiar significance to Shylock's words. 102. **spet:** spat.—**gaberdine:** a kind of long cloak or mantle. 105. **Go to then:** very well, then, very good, then. It is, however, used as a vague exclamation with many different meanings.

You that did void your rheum upon my beard
And foot me as you spurn a stranger cur
Over your threshold. Moneys is your suit.
What should I say to you? Should I not say   110
"Hath a dog money? Is it possible
A cur can lend three thousand ducats?" or
Shall I bend low, and in a bondman's key,
With bated breath and whisp'ring humbleness,
Say this: 115
"Fair sir, you spet on me on Wednesday last;
You spurn'd me such a day; another time
You call'd me dog; and for these courtesies
I'll lend you thus much moneys"?

ANT.   I am as like to call thee so again,   120
To spet on thee again, to spurn thee too.
If thou wilt lend this money, lend it not
As to thy friends—for when did friendship take
A breed for barren metal of his friend?
But lend it rather to thine enemy,   125
Who if he break, thou mayst with better face
Exact the penalty.

SHY.   Why, look you, how you storm!
I would be friends with you and have your love,
Forget the shames that you have stain'd me with,
Supply your present wants, and take no doit   130
Of usance for my moneys,
And you'll not hear me. This is kind I offer.

BASS.   This were kindness.

SHY.   This kindness will I show.
Go with me to a notary, seal me there
Your single bond; and, in a merry sport,   135
If you repay me not on such a day,
In such a place, such sum or sums as are
Express'd in the condition, let the forfeit
Be nominated for an equal pound
Of your fair flesh, to be cut off and taken   140
In what part of your body pleaseth me.

---

109. **Moneys is your suit.** The singular verb is common with a plural subject. 124. **A breed for barren metal.** Aristotle remarks that interest is against nature, since it is unnatural for gold and silver, which are barren, to have offspring. 126. **if he break:** if he become bankrupt. 130. **doit:** the smallest value, a fraction of a farthing. 133. **This were kindness.** *Were* is emphatic. 135. **Your single bond:** i.e., your bond without security. 139. **for.** We should say, "as."

ANT.	Content, in faith. I'll seal to such a bond, And say there is much kindness in the Jew.
BASS.	You shall not seal to such a bond for me! I'll rather dwell in my necessity. 145
ANT.	Why, fear not, man! I will not forfeit it. Within these two months—that's a month before This bond expires—I do expect return Of thrice three times the value of this bond.
SHY.	O father Abram, what these Christians are, 150 Whose own hard dealing teaches them suspect The thoughts of others! Pray you tell me this: If he should break his day, what should I gain By the exaction of the forfeiture? A pound of man's flesh taken from a man 155 Is not so estimable, profitable neither, As flesh of muttons, beefs, or goats. I say, To buy his favour I extend this friendship. If he will take it, so; if not, adieu; And for my love I pray you wrong me not. 160
ANT.	Yes, Shylock, I will seal unto this bond.
SHY.	Then meet me forthwith at the notary's; Give him direction for this merry bond, And I will go and purse the ducats straight, See to my house, left in the fearful guard 165 Of an unthrifty knave, and presently I will be with you.
ANT.	Hie thee, gentle Jew. *Exit* [Shylock]. The Hebrew will turn Christian; he grows kind.
BASS.	· I like not fair terms and a villain's mind.
ANT.	Come on. In this there can be no dismay; 170 My ships come home a month before the day. *Exeunt.*

---

142. **Content, in faith.** Antonio regards the Jew's proposition as kind, since he has no expectation of incurring the forfeiture. Shylock's conditions for the bond are horrible but his genial manner entraps Antonio into believing that Shylock for once intends to lend money without interest. 156. **Is not so estimable,** etc. worthwhile. 157. **muttons:** sheep—**beefs:** oxen. 158. **extend:** show. 159. **so:** very well. 160. **And for my love I pray you wrong me not:** i.e., in the future treat me more kindly, as I have proved a friend in this situation.. 165. **fearful:** dangerous, risky. 166. **knave:** servant—but with a suggestion of contempt. 169. **I like not fair terms...** Bassanio's proverbial quip nicely sums up the situation [K.R.].

Act II

Scene I. [*Belmont. Portia's house.*]†

Enter [the Prince of] Morocco, *a tawny Moor, all in white, and*
three or four Followers *accordingly, with* Portia, Nerissa, *and their* Train.

Mor.	Mislike me not for my complexion,	
	The shadowed livery of the burnish'd sun,	
	To whom I am a neighbour and near bred.	
	Bring me the fairest creature northward born,	
	Where Phœbus' fire scarce thaws the icicles,	5
	And let us make incision for your love	
	To prove whose blood is reddest, his or mine.	
	I tell thee, lady, this aspect of mine	
	Hath fear'd the valiant. By my love I swear,	
	The best-regarded virgins of our clime	10
	Have lov'd it too. I would not change this hue,	
	Except to steal your thoughts, my gentle queen.	
Por.	In terms of choice I am not solely led	
	By nice direction of a maiden's eyes.	
	Besides, the lott'ry of my destiny	15
	Bars me the right of voluntary choosing.	
	But, if my father had not scanted me,	
	And hedg'd me by his wit to yield myself	
	His wife who wins me by that means I told you,	
	Yourself, renowned Prince, then stood as fair	20

complexion

Act. II. Scene I.

1 ff. The Prince of Morocco's rhetoric reflects Shakespeare's attempt to capture the lush imagery of Arabic. Compare with *Othello*. 2. **The shadowed livery of the burnish'd sun.** His "tawny" complexion suggests brown rather than black as the livery which the servant wears signifies what lord he follows. *Livery* is often used, as here, in a figurative sense. *Shadowed* means "dark," literally "full of shadows." 8. **aspéct.** Accented on the second syllable. 9. **fear'd:** frightened. 13. **In terms of choice:** i.e., practically "in making my choice." *Terms* means "way or manner" and is frequently used pleonastically (redundantly) as here. 14. **nice direction:** foolish, as in a foolish adolescent girl's eye. In the next sentence she adds that she has not the right to choose, anyway. 18. **wit:** clever device. 20. **stood:** would stand.

---

†   Portia's Belmont villa in the Nunn version reflects in its minimalist décor some of the austerity in the personality of Derbhle Crotty, whose manner does not coincide with the kind of openness embodied in the Lynn Collins' Portia in the Radford version. This grand conception of the villa contrasts with the sparseness of Nunn's setting. [K.R.]

As any comer I have look'd on yet
For my affection.‡

MOR.   Even for that I thank you.
Therefore I pray you lead me to the caskets
To try my fortune. By this scimitar,
That slew the Sophy and a Persian prince   25
That won three fields of Sultan Solyman,
I would o'erstare the sternest eyes that look,
Outbrave the heart most daring on the earth,
Pluck the young sucking cubs from the she-bear,
Yea, mock the lion when 'a roars for prey,   30
To win thee, lady. But, alas the while!
If Hercules and Lichas play at dice
Which is the better man, the greater throw
May turn by fortune from the weaker hand:
So is Alcides beaten by his page,   35
And so may I, blind Fortune leading me,
Miss that which one unworthier may attain,
And die with grieving.

POR.   You must take your chance;
And either not attempt to choose at all,
Or swear before you choose, if you choose wrong, 40
Never to speak to lady afterward
In way of marriage. Therefore be advis'd.

MOR.   Nor will not. Come, bring me unto my chance.

POR.   First, forward to the temple; after dinner
Your hazard shall be made.

MOR.   Good fortune then!   45
To make me blest or cursed'st among men.   *Exeunt.*

---

31. **alas the while!** A common cry of sorrow or lamentation, something like today's "God help me!" 32. **Lichas:** the attendant of Hercules, as is explained in l. 35, where Alcides is Hercules. 42. **be advis'd:** consider carefully. 43. **Nor will not:** i.e., and I will never speak to a lady about marriage.

‡   Although *Merchant* is always thought of as a comedy, it nevertheless deals with the most precarious of emotions. Here Portia must stand by while the Prince of Morocco plays out her father's grim game of choosing a casket to seal their fates. In the Radford production, Lynn Collins as Portia shows the softer side of the Belmont heiress and comes across as kinder than either the Portia of Gemma Jones in the BBC version or of Derbhle Crotty in Nunn's production. [K.R.]

SCENE II. [*Venice. A street.*]

Enter [Launcelot] *the Clown, alone.*†

LAUN.   Certainly my conscience will serve me to run from this Jew my
master. The fiend is at mine elbow and tempts me, saying to me,
"Gobbo, Launcelot Gobbo, good Launcelot," or "good Gobbo," or
"good Launcelot Gobbo, use your legs, take the start, run away." My
conscience says, "No. Take heed, honest Launcelot; take heed, honest
Gobbo," or, as aforesaid, "honest Launcelot Gobbo, do not run; scorn
running with thy heels." Well, the most courageous fiend bids me
pack. "Via!" says the fiend. "Away!" says the fiend. "For the heavens,
rouse up a brave mind," says the fiend, "and run." Well, my conscience,
hanging about the neck of my heart, says very wisely to me, "My
honest friend Launcelot, being an honest man's son"—or rather an
honest woman's son; for indeed my father did something smack,
something grow to, he had a kind of taste—Well, my conscience says,
"Launcelot, budge not." "Budge," says the fiend. "Budge not," says
my conscience. "Conscience," say I, "you counsel well." "Fiend," say
I, "you counsel well." To be rul'd by my conscience, I should stay with
the Jew my master, who (God bless the mark!) is a kind of devil; and,
to run away from the Jew, I should be ruled by the fiend, who (saving
your reverence) is the devil himself. Certainly the Jew is the very devil
incarnation; and, in my conscience, my conscience is but a kind of
hard conscience to offer to counsel me to stay with the Jew. The fiend
gives the more friendly counsel. I will run, fiend; my heels are at your
commandment; I will run.   23

Enter Old Gobbo, *with a basket.*

SCENE II.

1ff. This entire passage has often been "filleted"or entirely cut by directors because of the fear that the
archaic language may be lost on modern audiences The speech actually draws on the morality play
tradition when a character is caught in a powerful moral contradiction. [K.R.]. 6-7. **scorn running with
thy heels.** A display of indignation [K.R.]. 8. **pack:** be off.—**Via.** Italian slang for "away," commonly
used among the Elizabethan English.—**For the heavens:** for Heaven's sake. 12. **something smack:**
i.e., a vice with a sexual innuendo. 13. **grow to:** have a tendency to.—**had a kind of taste.** More hints
that Old Gobbo was once a womanizer. 16. **To be ruled by:** i.e., if I were ruled by. 17. **God bless the
mark!** The meaning is uncertain, but often used, as here, to soften the shock of mentioning something
disagreeable. 18-19. **saving your reverence.** An adaptation of the Latin *salva reverentia,* "Due respect
being observed,"—an apologetic phrase, useful for laundering an ugly phrase into a polite conversation.
20. **incarnation:** incarnate. Gobbo's slip in language.

---

†   Launcelot's dilemma over conscience stems in part from the medieval morality play convention
when characters struggle between forces of good and evil, but one is also reminded of Hamlet's
deep concern about "conscience," which he thinks "does make cowards of us all." (*Hamlet* 3.1).
[K.R.]

GOB.   Master young man, you, I pray you, which is the way to Master Jew's?

LAUN.   [*aside*] O heavens, this is my truebegotten father! who, being more
            than sandblind, high-gravel-blind, knows me not. I will try confusions
            with him.   27

GOB.   Master young gentleman, I pray you which is the way to master Jew's?

LAUN.   Turn up on your right hand at the next turning, but, at the next
            turning of all, on your left; marry, at the very next turning, turn of no
            hand, but turn down indirectly to the Jew's house.   31

GOB.   Be God's sonties, 'twill be a hard way to hit! Can you tell me whether
            one Launcelot that dwells with him, dwell with him or no?

LAUN.   Talk you of young Master Launcelot? [*Aside*] Mark me now! Now will
            I raise the waters.—Talk you of young Master Launcelot?   35

GOB.   No master, sir, but a poor man's son. His father, though I say't, is an
            honest exceeding poor man, and, God be thanked, well to live.

LAUN.   Well, let his father be what 'a will, we talk of young Master Launcelot.

GOB.   Your worship's friend, and Launcelot, sir.

LAUN.   But, I pray you, ergo, old man, ergo, I beseech you, talk you of young
            Master Launcelot?   41

GOB.   Of Launcelot, an't please your mastership.

LAUN.   Ergo Master Launcelot. Talk not of Master Launcelot, father; for the
            young gentleman, according to Fates and Destinies and such odd
            sayings, the Sisters Three and such branches of learning, is indeed
            deceased, or, as you would say in plain terms, gone to heaven.   46

GOB.   Marry, God forbid! The boy was the very staff of my age, my very prop.

---

26. **sand-blind:** partially blind or rather, "dim-sighted." 32. **Be God's sonties.** An old popular oath,
the exact meaning of which was perhaps as murky to the Elizabethans as it is today. [K.R.].—**hit:** locate
34-35. **young Master Launcelot.** "Master" was the title for a very young gentleman.—**Now will I
raise the waters:** i.e., now will I stir up a commotion. 36. **No master, sir.** Old Gobbo vehemently
repudiates the gentleman's title of Master for his son. 37. **well to live:** well off in this world's goods.
An obvious contradiction of what precedes, and of course intentional on Shakespeare's part, since he
represents Old Gobbo as somewhat confused. 38. **let his father be what a' will.** Launcelot speaks in
a lofty tone, as if the subject of Launcelot's father were of no consequence. *A'* is a colloquial, abraded
form of *he*. 39. **Your worship's friend, and Launcelot, sir.** Gobbo corrects the phrase "young Master
Launcelot," and describes his son as one who would be glad to be a friend to the young gentleman with
whom he is now speaking, but who should be called plain *Launcelot* without any *Master*. 40. **ergo:**
therefore—a common term used in formal logical reasoning, as in the schools. 42. **an't:** if it. 43. **father.**
The use of this term does not disclose Launcelot's identity to Old Gobbo, since *father* was a common
form of address from young men to old, even when there was no relationship. 44-45. **such odd sayings.**
Launcelot is doing his best to affect an offhand, quasi-learned manner, as he supposes would be the style
of a young gentleman..—**the Sisters Three:** the Fates.

LAUN.	[*aside*] Do I look like a cudgel or a hovel-post, a staff, or a prop?—Do you know me, father? 49
GOB.	Alack the day, I know you not, young gentleman! but I pray you tell me, is my boy (God rest his soul!) alive or dead?
LAUN.	Do you not know me, father?
GOB.	Alack, sir, I am sand-blind! I know you not. 53
LAUN.	Nay, indeed, if you had your eyes, you might fail of the knowing me. It is a wise father that knows his own child. Well, old man, I will tell you news of your son. [*Kneels.*] Give me your blessing. Truth will come to light; murder cannot be hid long—a man's son may, but in the end truth will out. 58
GOB.	Pray you, sir, stand up. I am sure you are not Launcelot, my boy.
LAUN.	Pray you let's have no more fooling about it, but give me your blessing. I am Launcelot—your boy that was, your son that is, your child that shall be. 62
GOB.	I cannot think you are my son.
LAUN.	I know not what I shall think of that; but I am Launcelot, the Jew's man, and I am sure Margery your wife is my mother.
GOB.	Her name is Margery indeed. I'll be sworn, if thou be Launcelot, thou art mine own flesh and blood. Lord worshipp'd might he be! What a beard hast thou got! Thou hast got more hair on thy chin than Dobbin my fill-horse has on his tail. 69
LAUN.	[*rises*] It should seem then that Dobbin's tail grows backward. I am sure he had more hair of his tail than I have of my face when I last saw him.
GOB.	Lord, how art thou chang'd! How dost thou and thy master agree? I have brought him a present. How 'gree you now? 73
LAUN.	Well, well; but, for mine own part, as I have set up my rest to run away, so I will not rest till I have run some ground. My master's a very

---

48-49. **Do you know me, father?** Here Launcelot tries to disclose himself to the old man, but at first without success. 51. **God rest his soul.** Only appropriate of course to one who is dead. 55. **It is a wise father,** etc. Launcelot's variation of the proverb "'Tis a wise child that knows his own father." 56. **Give me your blessing.** As he says this, Launcelot kneels to the old man. 64. **I know not what I shall think of that:** i.e., I don't know what to think about being your son, according of course to the proverb that "'Tis a wise child that knows his own father" referred to above. 67-68. **Lord worshipp'd might he be! What a beard hast thou got!** In an old stage tradition, Launcelot turns the back of his head to his father's hand so that his father thinks his long hair is a beard. 69. **fill-horse.** A *fill-horse* or *thill-horse* was a cart-horse used in hauling dirt or debris. 71. **of:** on. 74-75. **I have set up my rest to run away:** I have made up my mind to run away, an idiom adopted from the game of cards known as primero, in which a player satisfied to take his stand, as it were, on the cards he held said, "I set up my rest."—**some ground:** some distance.

Jew. Give him a present? Give him a halter! I am famish'd in his service. You may tell every finger I have with my ribs. Father, I am glad you are come. Give me your present to one Master Bassanio, who indeed gives rare new liveries. If I serve not him, I will run as far as God has any ground. O rare fortune! here comes the man. To him, father; for I am a Jew if I serve the Jew any longer.   81

Enter Bassanio, *with* [Leonardo and] *a Follower or two.*

BASS. You may do so; but let it be so hasted that supper be ready at the farthest by five of the clock. See these letters delivered, put the liveries to making, and desire Gratiano to come anon to my lodging.
Exit one of his men.

LAUN. To him, father.   85

GOB.   God bless your worship!

BASS. Gramercy. Wouldst thou aught with me?

GOB.   Here's my son, sir, a poor boy—

LAUN. Not a poor boy, sir, but the rich Jew's man, that would, sir, as my father shall specify—   90

GOB.   He hath a great infection, sir, as one would say, to serve—

LAUN. Indeed, the short and the long is, I serve the Jew, and have a desire, as my father shall specify—

GOB.   His master and he (saving your worship's reverence) are scarce cater-cousins.   95

LAUN. To be brief, the very truth is, that the Jew having done me wrong, doth cause me, as my father, being, I hope, an old man, shall frutify unto you—

GOB.   I have here a dish of doves that I would bestow upon your worship; and my suit is—   100

LAUN. In very brief, the suit is impertinent to myself, as your worship shall know by this honest old man; and, though I say it, though old man, yet poor man, my father.

---

77. **tell:** count. 79-80. **as far as God has any ground:** as far as the end of the world.—**To him, father:** i.e., go to him, father. 82. **You may do so.** Bassanio is assenting to some suggestion made by his servant, Leonardo. 87. **Gramercy.** A corruption of "grant mercy," i.e., a French phrase for "great thanks." 91. **infection.** Old Gobbo's attempts to use fine language trap him into sounding like Mrs. Malaprop [K.R.]. He means "affection" or "desire." 94-95. **saving your worship's reverence.** A respectful phrase like "saving your reverence" in l. 18, above.—**scarce cater-cousins:** i.e., they are anything but intimate friends like "cater-cousins," persons so close that they "cater" to, serve, each other [K.R.]. 97. **frutify.** Launcelot's mistake for *fructify,* which again would be his blunder for *notify* or *signify.* 101. **impertinent.** Launcelot's mistake for *appurtenant.*

BASS.	One speak for both. What would you?	
LAUN.	Serve you, sir.	105
GOB.	That is the very defect of the matter, sir.	
BASS.	I know thee well; thou hast obtain'd thy suit.	
	Shylock thy master spoke with me this day	
	And hath preferr'd thee, if it be preferment	
	To leave a rich Jew's service to become	110
	The follower of so poor a gentleman.	
LAUN.	The old proverb is very well parted between my master Shylock and	
	you, sir. You have the grace of God, sir, and he hath enough.	
BASS.	Thou speak'st it well. Go, father, with thy son.	
	Take leave of thy old master and enquire	115
	My lodging out. [*To a Servant*] Give him a livery	
	More guarded than his fellows'. See it done.	
LAUN.	Father, in. I cannot get a service, no! I have ne'er a tongue in my head!	
	Well, [looks on his palm] if any man in Italy have a fairer table which	
	doth offer to swear upon a book—! I shall have good fortune. Go to,	
	here's a simple line of life! Here's a small trifle of wives! Alas, fifteen	
	wives is nothing! a 'leven widows and nine maids is a simple coming-in	
	for one man; and then to scape drowning thrice, and to be in peril of	
	my life with the edge of a featherbed! Here are simple scapes. Well, if	
	Fortune be a woman, she's a good wench for this gear. Father, come.	
	I'll take my leave of the Jew in the twinkling.	126

Exit [*with Old Gobbo*].

BASS.	I pray thee, good Leonardo, think on this:	
	These things being bought and orderly bestow'd	

---

106. **defect:** Gobbo's mistake for *effect*, i.e., *upshot*. 109. **preferr'd thee:** recommended thee to advancement. 112. **The old proverb.** The proverb is "He that hath the grace of God, hath enough." A part of it applies, says Launcelot, to Shylock, a part to Bassanio. 114. **father.** Note how Bassanio addresses the old man as "father" out of respect. 117. **More guarded:** more trimmed. Launcelot is a fantastic person and Bassanio intends to make a show of him. 118. **in:** enter.—**I cannot get a service, no.** Said with lofty irony. 119-120. **Well...a fairer table.** Here Sir Thomas Hanmer [18th-century editor of Shakespeare] inserts a stage direction, "Looking on his own hand." This reference to Palmistry is certainly right as Launcelot thinks that the lines in his hand mark him out as a favorite of fortune .—**which doth offer to swear upon a book.** In one form of oath it was customary to lay the hand upon the Bible.—**Go to:** well, well. Launcelot proceeds to examine the various lines in his hand. One of these is known as the line of life, another as the line of marriage. According to his reading of the latter, he is to have fifteen wives, eleven of them widows. 122. **a simple coming-in:** a mere trifle in the way of income. Perhaps he expects to get dowries or fortunes with all these wives. 123. **to scape drowning,** etc. Launcelot still pretends to be reading the fortune predicted by the lines in his hands. 124. **Here are simple scapes:** mere trifles in the way of escapes—said, of course, with lofty irony. 125. **for this gear:** for this business, i.e., this favor that he has done me in allowing me to leave the Jew's service for Bassanio's. The reference may be also to the whole fortunate history that he has read in the palm of his hand. 128. **bestow'd:** put away in safety.

	Return in haste, for I do feast tonight	
	My best-esteem'd acquaintance. Hie thee, go.	130
LEON.	My best endeavours shall be done herein.	

Enter Gratiano.

GRA.	Where 's your master?	
LEON.	Yonder, sir, he walks.	*Exit.*
GRA.	Signior Bassanio!	
BASS.	Gratiano!	
GRA.	I have a suit to you.	
BASS.	You have obtain'd it.	135
GRA.	You must not deny me. I must go with you	
	To Belmont.	
BASS.	Why, then you must. But hear thee, Gratiano.	
	Thou art too wild, too rude, and bold of voice—	
	Parts that become thee happily enough	140
	And in such eyes as ours appear not faults;	
	But where thou art not known, why, there they show	
	Something too liberal. Pray thee take pain	
	To allay with some cold drops of modesty	
	Thy skipping spirit, lest through thy wild behavior	145
	I be misconst'red in the place I go to	
	And lose my hopes.	
GRA.	Signior Bassanio, hear me.	
	If I do not put on a sober habit,	
	Talk with respect, and swear but now and then,	
	Wear prayer books in my pocket, look demurely,	150
	Nay more, while grace is saying hood mine eyes	
	Thus with my hat, and sigh, and say amen,	
	Use all the observance of civility	
	Like one well studied in a sad ostent	
	To please his grandam, never trust me more.	155
BASS.	Well, we shall see your bearing.	
GRA.	Nay, but I bar tonight. You shall not gauge me	
	By what we do tonight.	
BASS.	No, that were pity.	

[handwritten margin note:] to outwit/trick the women by dressing or acting in certain ways

---

140. **Parts:** personality traits. 142. **show:** appear. 143. **liberal:** free.—**take pain:** take pains. 144. **modesty:** moderation. 154. **one well studied in a sad ostent:** a person who has taken pains to adopt a sober and serious appearance.

I would entreat you rather to put on
Your boldest suit of mirth, for we have friends   160
That purpose merriment. But fare you well.
I have some business.

GRA.   And I must to Lorenzo and the rest;
But we will visit you at supper time.   *Exeunt.*

SCENE III. [*Venice. Shylock's house.*]

Enter Jessica *and* [Launcelot] *the Clown.*

JES.   I am sorry thou wilt leave my father so.
Our house is hell; and thou, a merry devil,
Didst rob it of some taste of tediousness.
But fare thee well. There is a ducat for thee;
And, Launcelot, soon at supper shalt thou see   5
Lorenzo, who is thy new master's guest.
Give him this letter; do it secretly;
And so farewell. I would not have my father
See me in talk with thee.

LAUN.   Adieu! Tears exhibit my tongue. Most beautiful pagan, most sweet Jew!
if a Christian did not play the knave and get thee, I am much deceived.
But adieu! These foolish drops do something drown my manly spirit.
Adieu!   13

JES.   Farewell, good Launcelot.   *Exit* [*Launcelot*].
Alack, what heinous sin is it in me
To be asham'd to be my father's child!   child of jew
But though I am a daughter to his blood,
I am not to his manners. O Lorenzo,
If thou keep promise, I shall end this strife,
Become a Christian and thy loving wife.   *Exit.*   20

159-60. **to put on Your boldest suit of mirth.** Shakespeare is fond of figures from clothing, especially those dressing characters in clothing appropriate to their style.
SCENE III.
5. **soon at supper:** at supper tonight. 10. **exhibit.** Launcelot's mistake for "inhibit," i.e., check, restrain. 12. **These foolish drops.** Launcelot, who endeavors to speak like a gentleman, uses the regular Elizabethan euphemism for tears. 18. **his manners:** his character—like the Latin *mores.* 19-20. Scenes often terminate with a closed couplet, as here.

A quarrel between Jessica (Gabrielle Jourdan) and Shylock (Henry Goodman) terminates in an ugly moment when he slaps her face. A stricken Jessica cries out, "O Lorenzo /... I shall end this strife, / Become a Christian and thy loving wife." (Nunn, 2001)

SCENE IV. [*Venice. A street.*]

Enter Gratiano, Lorenzo, Salerio, *and* Solanio.

LOR.   Nay, we will slink away in supper time,
        Disguise us at my lodging, and return
        All in an hour.

GRA.   We have not made good preparation.

SALER. We have not spoke us yet of torchbearers.   5

SOLAN. 'Tis vile, unless it may be quaintly ordered,
        And better in my mind not undertook.

LOR.   'Tis now but four o'clock. We have two hours
        To furnish us.

                Enter Launcelot, *with a letter.*

        Friend Launcelot, what's the news?

LAUN.   An it shall please you to break up this, it shall seem to signify.   10

SCENE IV.
1. **in supper time:** during supper. 5. **We have not spoke us yet of torchbearers:** i.e., we have not adequately explored how to hire torchbearers.—**torchbearers.** Always used in connection with masques and other fetes. 6. **quaintly ordered:** meticulously planned with due attention to detail. 10. **break up:** open.—**it shall seem to signify:** it will probably give you the information you require. Pleonasm (repetitive use of language to say the same thing) was common in Elizabethan English.

LOR.   I know the hand. In faith, 'tis a fair hand, *woman*
       And whiter than the paper it writ on
       Is the fair hand that writ.

GRA.   Love-news, in faith!

LAUN. By your leave, sir.

LOR.   Whither goest thou?   15

LAUN. Marry, sir, to bid my old master the Jew to sup tonight with my new
       master the Christian.

LOR.   Hold here, take this [*gives money*]. Tell gentle Jessica
       I will not fail her. Speak it privately.
       Go. [*Exit Launcelot.*] Gentlemen,   20
       Will you prepare you for this masque tonight?
       I am provided of a torchbearer.

SALER. Ay, marry, I'll be gone about it straight.

SOLAN. And so will I.

LOR.   Meet me and Gratiano
       At Gratiano's lodging some hour hence.   25

SALER. 'Tis good we do so.   *Exeunt [Salerio and Solanio].*

GRA.   Was not that letter from fair Jessica?

LOR.   I must needs tell thee all. She hath directed
       How I shall take her from her father's house;
       What gold and jewels she is furnish'd with;   30
       What page's suit she hath in readiness.
       If e'er the Jew her father come to heaven,
       It will be for his gentle daughter's sake;
       And never dare misfortune cross her foot,
       Unless she do it under this excuse,   35
       That she is issue to a faithless Jew.
       Come, go with me; peruse this as thou goest.
       Fair Jessica shall be my torchbearer.   *Exeunt.*

homoerotic
torch bearer

---

14. **By your leave, sir.** Asking permission to depart. 16. **to bid:** to invite. 18. **take this.** Giving him a present or a token. 22. **a torchbearer.** Each masquerader was regularly accompanied by one torchbearer. 25. **some hour:** about an hour. 34. **cross her foot:** cross her path. 36. **faithless:** unbelieving, infidel. 38. **Fair Jessica shall be my torchbearer:** i.e., in disguise.

SCENE V. [*Venice. Before Shylock's house.*]

Enter [the] Jew [Shylock] and [Launcelot,] his man that was the Clown.

SHY.	Well, thou shalt see, thy eyes shall be thy judge,
	The difference of old Shylock and Bassanio.—
	What, Jessica!—Thou shalt not gormandize
	As thou hast done with me—What, Jessica!—
	And sleep, and snore, and rend apparel out.—

5

Why, Jessica, I say!

LAUN.   Why, Jessica!

SHY.   Who bids thee call? I do not bid thee call.

LAUN.   Your worship was wont to tell me I could do nothing without bidding.

Enter Jessica.

JES.   Call you? What is your will?

SHY.   I am bid forth to supper, Jessica.   10
         There are my keys. But wherefore should I go?
         I am not bid for love; they flatter me.
         But yet I'll go in hate, to feed upon
         The prodigal Christian. Jessica, my girl,†
         Look to my house. I am right loath to go.   15
         There is some ill a-brewing towards my rest,
         For I did dream of money bags tonight.

LAUN.   I beseech you, sir, go. My young master doth expect your reproach.

SHY.   So do I his.   19

LAUN.   And they have conspired together. I will not say you shall see a masque;
         but if you do, then it was not for nothing that my nose fell a-bleeding
         on Black Monday last at six o'clock i' th' morning, falling out that year
         on Ash Wednesday was four year in th' afternoon.   23

SCENE V.
3. **What, Jessica.** A nagging call to his daughter. 6. **Why.** Another nagging call 10. **bid forth:** invite out. 17. **I did dream of money bags.** Dreams go by contraries, according to the proverb; hence Shylock's dream portends misfortune. 18. **reproach.** Launcelot's mistake for *approach.* 19. **So do I his.** Shylock replies as if Launcelot had used *reproach* in its proper sense, as he expects only hostility from Bassanio. 20. **And:** possibly if, though with the period after *together* and can be construed in its ordinary sense. 21. **my nose fell a-bleeding:** an omen of ill luck. 22. **Black Monday:** Easter Monday. 23. **Ash Wednesday was four year:** i.e., four years ago last Ash Wednesday.

---

†   In the Nunn production Shylock and Jessica sing a duet, "Eshet Chavil," a Hebrew song honoring the contributions of women to domestic tranquility. While obviously extratextual, the song shows a warmth and humanity in Shylock usually hidden from view. [K.R.]

SHY.	What, are there masques? Hear you me, Jessica.	
	Lock up my doors; and when you hear the drum	25
	And the vile squealing of the wry-neck'd fife,	
	Clamber not you up to the casements then,	
	Nor thrust your head into the public street	
	To gaze on Christian fools with varnish'd faces;	
	But stop my house's ears—I mean my casements.	30
	Let not the sound of shallow fopp'ry enter	
	My sober house. By Jacob's staff I swear	
	I have no mind of feasting forth tonight;	
	But I will go. Go you before me, sirrah.	
	Say I will come.	35
LAUN.	I will go before, sir. Mistress, look out at window for all this.	
	There will come a Christian by	
	Will be worth a Jewess' eye. [*Exit.*]	
SHY.	What says that fool of Hagar's offspring? ha?	
JES.	His words were "Farewell, mistress"—nothing else.	40
SHY.	The patch is kind enough, but a huge feeder,	
	Snail-slow in profit, and he sleeps by day	
	More than the wildcat. Drones hive not with me;	
	Therefore I part with him, and part with him	
	To one that I would have him help to waste	45
	His borrowed purse. Well, Jessica, go in.	
	Perhaps I will return immediately.	
	Do as I bid you; shut doors after you.	
	Fast bind, fast find—	
	A proverb never stale in thrifty mind. *Exit.*	50
JES.	Farewell; and if my fortune be not crost,	
	I have a father, you a daughter, lost. *Exit*	

---

26. **wry-necked fife.** Often so named because of the position of the player's head. 27. **casements:** windows. 29. **varnish'd faces:** faces covered with varnished masks. 31. **fopp'ry:** foolishness. 33. **I have no mind of feasting forth tonight.** In yet another example of Shakespeare's liking for premonition, Shylock feels a disaster approaching. 36. **Mistress, look out at window.** Launcelot is conveying his private message to Jessica, in accordance with Lorenzo's request at 2.4.19. 39. **of Hagar's offspring:** i.e., Hagar with her son Ishmael was cast into the desert by Abraham. 41. **patch:** fool. 42. **in profit:** i.e., in doing anything profitable. 43. **wildcat:** which sleeps by day and prowls by night.

Scene VI. [*Venice. Near Shylock's house.*]

Enter the Maskers, Gratiano *and* Salerio.

GRA.   This is the penthouse under which Lorenzo
          Desir'd us to make stand.

SALER.   His hour is almost past.

GRA.   And it is marvel he outdwells his hour,
          For lovers ever run before the clock.

SALER.   O, ten times faster Venus' pigeons fly   5
          To seal love's bonds new-made than they are wont
          To keep obliged faith unforfeited!

GRA.   That ever holds. Who riseth from a feast
          With that keen appetite that he sits down?
          Where is the horse that doth untread again   10
          His tedious measures with the unbated fire
          That he did pace them first? All things that are
          Are with more spirit chased than enjoy'd.
          How like a younker or a prodigal
          The scarfed bark puts from her native bay,   15
          Hugg'd and embraced by the strumpet wind!
          How like the Prodigal doth she return,
          With over-weather'd ribs and ragged sails,
          Lean, rent, and beggar'd by the strumpet wind!

Enter Lorenzo.

SALER.   Here comes Lorenzo. More of this hereafter.   20

LOR.   Sweet friends, your patience for my long abode.
          Not I, but my affairs, have made you wait.
          When you shall please to play the thieves for wives,
          I'll watch as long for you then. Approach.
          Here dwells my father Jew. Ho! who's within?   25

[Enter] Jessica, *above, [in boy's clothes].*

SCENE VI.
1. **penthouse:** a lean-to. The word was pronounced *pentus*. Ben Jonson rhymes it with *juventus*. 5.
Venus' pigeons. Sacred doves were thought to draw Venus' chariot 7. **obliged:** pledged. 11. **His
tedious measures.** Horses trained to go through elaborate show steps. *Measure* was regularly used
for a stately dance.—**unbated:** unabated. 14. **younker.** Properly, "a young gentleman"; then "a frisky
youth." 15. **scarfed:** adorned with pennants and streamers. 18. **over-weather'd:** battered and stained
by the weather.

JES.   Who are you? Tell me for more certainty,
             Albeit I'll swear that I do know your tongue.

LOR.   Lorenzo, and thy love.

JES.   Lorenzo certain, and my love indeed,
             For who love I so much? And now who knows   30
             But you, Lorenzo, whether I am yours?

LOR.   Heaven and thy thoughts are witness that thou art.

JES.   Here, catch this casket; it is worth the pains.
             I am glad 'tis night, you do not look on me,
             For I am much asham'd of my exchange.   35
             But love is blind, and lovers cannot see
             The pretty follies that themselves commit;
             For if they could, Cupid himself would blush
             To see me thus transformed to a boy.

LOR.   Descend, for you must be my torchbearer.   40

JES.   What, must I hold a candle to my shames?
             They in themselves, good sooth, are too too light.
             Why, 'tis an office of discovery, love,
             And I should be obscur'd.

LOR.   So are you, sweet,
             Even in the lovely garnish of a boy.   45
             But come at once;
             For the close night doth play the runaway,
             And we are stay'd for at Bassanio's feast.

JES.   I will make fast the doors, and gild myself
             With some moe ducats, and be with you straight.   [Exit above.] 50

GRA.   Now, by my hood, a gentle, and no Jew!

LOR.   Beshrow me but I love her heartily;
             For she is wise, if I can judge of her;
             And fair she is, if that mine eyes be true;
             And true she is, as she hath prov'd herself;   55
             And therefore, like herself, wise, fair, and true,
             Shall she be placed in my constant soul.

                        Enter Jessica, [*below*].

---

35. **my exchange:** i.e., my change of clothes. 42. **too too light:** too frivolous. The repetition of *too* was a common Elizabethan idiom. 43. **'tis an office of discovery:** a torchbearer by his conspicuousness is vulnerable to quick discovery. 44. **obscur'd:** kept hidden. 45. **garnish:** attire. 47. **close:** secret, i.e., favorable to concealment. 50. **Moe:** more. 52. **Beshrow me but:** curse me unless. *Beshrew*, however, is a very mild word, though its literal meaning is as here given.

What, art thou come? On, gentlemen! away!
Our masquing mates by this time for us stay.

Exit [with Jessica and Salerio].

Enter Antonio.

ANT.   Who's there?   60

GRA.   Signior Antonio?

ANT.   Fie, fie, Gratiano! Where are all the rest?
'Tis nine o'clock; our friends all stay for you.
No masque tonight. The wind is come about;
Bassanio presently will go aboard.   65
I have sent twenty out to seek for you.

GRA.   I am glad on't. I desire no more delight
Than to be under sail and gone tonight.   *Exeunt.*

SCENE VII. [*Belmont. Portia's house.*]†

Enter Portia, *with* Morocco, *and both their* Trains.

POR.   Go, draw aside the curtains and discover
The several caskets to this noble Prince.
Now make your choice.   [*The curtains are drawn aside.*]

MOR.   The first, of gold, which this inscription bears,
"Who chooseth me shall gain what many men desire."   5
The second, silver, which this promise carries,
"Who chooseth me shall get as much as he deserves."
This third, dull lead, with warning all as blunt,
"Who chooseth me must give and hazard all he hath."
How shall I know if I do choose the right?   10

POR.   The one of them contains my picture, Prince.
If you choose that, then I am yours withal.

---

65. **presently:** instantly.
SCENE VII.
1. **discover:** disclose. 5. **Who chooseth,** etc. The inscriptions in formal Alexandrines on the caskets set them off from the dramatic blank verse characteristic of the rest of the play. 8. **as blunt:** i.e., as blunt as the lead is. 12. **withal:** with it, at the same time.

---

†   The casket scene has inspired scene designers to invent appropriate settings for what turns out to be a quasi-religious rite. In stage and film versions the caskets come in all sizes and shapes, from enormous objects that need to be levitated to Lilliputian curio-sized vessels. In the BBC version the king-sized variety emerges, while in the Nunn the mini-sized caskets echo the minimalist motifs of the set design. Here Morocco makes the crushing discovery that "All that glisters is not gold." [K.R.]

MOR.   Some god direct my judgment! Let me see.
         I will survey th' inscriptions back again.
         What says this leaden casket?   15
         "Who chooseth me must give and hazard all he hath."
         Must give—for what? for lead! hazard for lead?
         This casket threatens. Men that hazard all
         Do it in hope of fair advantages.
         A golden mind stoops not to shows of dross.   20
         I'll then nor give nor hazard aught for lead.
         What says the silver, with her virgin hue? *white*
         "Who chooseth me shall get as much as he deserves."
         As much as he deserves? Pause there, Morocco,
         And weigh thy value with an even hand.   25
         If thou beest rated by thy estimation,
         Thou dost deserve enough; and yet enough
         May not extend so far as to the lady;
         And yet to be afeard of my deserving
         Were but a weak disabling of myself.   30
         As much as I deserve? Why, that's the lady!
         I do in birth deserve her, and in fortunes,
         In graces, and in qualities of breeding;
         But more than these, in love I do deserve.
         What if I stray'd no farther, but chose here?   35
         Let's see once more this saying grav'd in gold:
         "Who chooseth me shall gain what many men desire."
         Why, that's the lady! All the world desires her.
         From the four corners of the earth they come
         To kiss this shrine, this mortal breathing saint.   40
         The Hyrcanian deserts and the vasty wilds
         Of wide Arabia are as throughfares now
         For princes to come view fair Portia.
         The watery kingdom, whose ambitious head
         Spets in the face of heaven, is no bar   45
         To stop the foreign spirits; but they come,
         As o'er a brook, to see fair Portia.
         One of these three contains her heavenly picture.
         Is't like that lead contains her? 'Twere damnation

---

14. **back again:** i.e., from last to first, in reverse order. 20. **shows of dross:** worthless appearances. *Dross* is used for any base metal. 22. **her virgin hue.** Silver is the color of the moon, and Diana, the virgin goddess, is the moon goddess. 26. **rated by thy estimation:** valued in accordance with thy reputation. 30. **disabling:** disprizing, undervaluing. 33. **graces:** pleasing qualities.—**qualities:** accomplishments. 42. **throughfares:** thoroughfares. 44-45. **The watery kingdom,** etc. This strong hyperbole (exaggeration) is adapted to the Prince's flamboyant language. *The watery kingdom* is the sea. 46. **spirits:** spirited persons.

To think so base a thought. It were too gross   50
To rib her cerecloth in the obscure grave.
Or shall I think in silver she's immur'd,
Being ten times undervalued to tried gold?
O sinful thought! Never so rich a gem
Was set in worse than gold. They have in England   55
A coin that bears the figure of an angel
Stamped in gold—but that's insculp'd upon;
But here an angel in a golden bed
Lies all within. Deliver me the key.
Here do I choose, and thrive I as I may!   60

POR.   There, take it, Prince; and if my form lie there,
         Then I am yours.   [*He opens the golden casket.*]

MOR.   skull   O hell! what have we here?
         A carrion Death, within whose empty eye
         There is a written scroll! I'll read the writing.
         "All that glisters is not gold—   65
         Often have you heard that told.
         Many a man his life hath sold
         But my outside to behold.
         Gilded tombs do worms infold.
         Had you been as wise as bold,   70
         Young in limbs, in judgment old,
         Your answer had not been inscroll'd.
         Fare you well; your suit is cold."
         Cold indeed, and labour lost.
         Then farewell heat, and welcome frost!   75
         Portia, adieu. I have too griev'd a heart
         To take a tedious leave. Thus losers part.   *Exit* [*with his Train*].

POR.   A gentle riddance. Draw the curtains, go.
         Let all of his complexion choose me so.   *Exeunt.*

---

50. **gross:** coarse, valueless. 51. **To rib her cerecloth:** i.e., to wrap in lead the waxed cloth in which her body lies.—**óbscure:** dark, with accentuation on the first syllable. 53. **ten times.** Gold was then ten times as valuable as silver. 56. **an angel:** the coin known by this name, inscribed with the figure of an angel. 57. **insculp'd:** sculptured. 58. **an angel:** i.e., Portia's portrait. 60. **thrive I as I may!** let me have what fortune I can get. 63. **A carrion death.** Cf. Greene, *Mamillia* (ed. Grosart, II. 114): "he which maketh choyce of bewty without vertue commits as much folly as *Critius* did, in choosing a golden boxe filled with rotten bones." 65. **All that glisters is not gold.** A common proverb long before Shakespeare's time. 68. **oútside.** accent on the first syllable. 72. **inscroll'd:** written on this scroll. The answer in question is given in the next verse. 75. **farewell heat, and welcome frost.** Since the Prince, according to his vow, must never take a wife, he bids farewell to love. 77. **Thus losers part:** i.e., abruptly, without any ceremonious leave-taking. 79. **so:** i.e., unsuccessfully, as he has done.

SCENE VIII. [*Venice. A street.*]

Enter Salerio *and* Solanio.

SALER. Why, man, I saw Bassanio under sail;
With him is Gratiano gone along;
And in their ship I am sure Lorenzo is not.

SOLAN. The villain Jew with outcries rais'd the Duke,
Who went with him to search Bassanio's ship.   5

SALER. He came too late, the ship was under sail;
But there the Duke was given to understand
That in a gondilo were seen together
Lorenzo and his amorous Jessica.
Besides, Antonio certified the Duke   10
They were not with Bassanio in his ship.

SOLAN. I never heard a passion so confus'd,
So strange, outrageous, and so variable,
As the dog Jew did utter in the streets.
"My daughter! O my ducats! O my daughter!   15
Fled with a Christian! O my Christian ducats!   *ducats = daughter*
Justice! the law! My ducats, and my daughter!
A sealed bag, two sealed bags of ducats,
Of double ducats, stol'n from me by my daughter!
And jewels—two stones, two rich and precious stones,   20
Stol'n by my daughter! Justice! Find the girl!
She hath the stones upon her, and the ducats!"

SALER. Why, all the boys in Venice follow him,
Crying his stones, his daughter, and his ducats.

SOLAN. Let good Antonio look he keep his day,   25
Or he shall pay for this.

SALER.   Marry, well remem'bred.
I reason'd with a Frenchman yesterday,
Who told me, in the narrow seas that part
The French and English there miscarried
A vessel of our country richly fraught.   30
I thought upon Antonio when he told me,
And wish'd in silence that it were not his.

SCENE VIII.
12. **passion:** fit of emotion. 25. **keep his day:** i.e., promptly repay the money that he has borrowed from Shylock. 27. **reason'd:** conversed. 29. **miscarried:** was lost. 30. **fraught:** freighted.

SOLAN. You were best to tell Antonio what you hear.
        Yet do not suddenly, for it may grieve him.

SALER. A kinder gentleman treads not the earth.   35
        I saw Bassanio and Antonio part.
        Bassanio told him he would make some speed
        Of his return; he answered, "Do not so.
        Slubber not business for my sake, Bassanio,
        But stay the very riping of the time;   40
        And for the Jew's bond which he hath of me,
        Let it not enter in your mind of love.
        Be merry, and employ your chiefest thoughts
        To courtship, and such fair ostents of love
        As shall conveniently become you there."   45
        And even there, his eye being big with tears,
        Turning his face, he put his hand behind him,
        And with affection wondrous sensible
        He wrung Bassanio's hand; and so they parted.

SOLAN. I think he only loves the world for him.   50
        I pray thee let us go and find him out,
        And quicken his embraced heaviness
        With some delight or other.

SALER.   Do we so.   *Exeunt.*

SCENE IX. [*Belmont. Portia's house.*]

Enter Nerissa *and a* Servitor.

NER.   Quick, quick, I pray thee; draw the curtain straight.
        The Prince of Arragon hath ta'en his oath
        And comes to his election presently.

        Enter Arragon, *his Train, and* Portia [*with her Train*].

POR.   Behold, there stand the caskets, noble Prince.
        If you choose that wherein I am contain'd,   5

---

33. **You were best.** You would be well advised 39. **Slubber.** Literally, "to soil or stain"; the same word as *slobber*, but often meaning "to perform carelessly," "to botch or bungle anything." Antonio requests Bassanio to take the time necessary for the successful outcome of his suit. 41. **for:** as for. 42. **your mind of love:** your loving mind. 44. **ostents:** shows, exhibitions. 45. **conveniently:** fittingly. 46. **big with** full of. 48. **affection wondrous sensible:** deeply felt emotion or love. 52. **quicken his embraced heaviness:** cure his melancholy by cheering him up.

SCENE IX.
3. **election:** choice.—**presently:** immediately.

Straight shall our nuptial rites be solemniz'd;
But if you fail, without more speech, my lord,
You must be gone from hence immediately.

ARR.   I am enjoin'd by oath to observe three things:
First, never to unfold to any one   10
Which casket 'twas I chose; next, if I fail
Of the right casket, never in my life
To woo a maid in way of marriage;
Lastly,
If I do fail in fortune of my choice,   15
Immediately to leave you and be gone.

POR.   To these injunctions every one doth swear
That comes to hazard for my worthless self.

ARR.   And so have I address'd me. Fortune now
To my heart's hope! Gold, silver, and base lead.   20
"Who chooseth me must give and hazard all he hath."
You shall look fairer ere I give or hazard.
What says the golden chest? Ha, let me see!
"Who chooseth me shall gain what many men desire."
What many men desire! That "many" may be meant   25
By the fool multitude, that choose by show,
Not learning more than the fond eye doth teach;
Which pries not to th' interior, but, like the martlet,
Builds in the weather on the outward wall,
Even in the force and road of casualty.   30
I will not choose what many men desire,
Because I will not jump with common spirits
And rank me with the barbarous multitude,
Why then, to thee, thou silver treasure house!
Tell me once more what title thou dost bear.   35
"Who chooseth me shall get as much as he deserves."
And well said too; for who shall go about
To cozen fortune, and be honorable
Without the stamp of merit? Let none presume
To wear an undeserved dignity.   40
O that estates, degrees, and offices
Were not deriv'd corruptly, and that clear honor

---

19. **so I have address'd me:** I have studied the stipulations and agree to them. 26. **By:** concerning. 27. **fond:** foolish. 28. **martlet:** martin—the "temple-haunting" bird mentioned by Banquo as building its nest on Macbeth's castle (1.6). 30. **in the force,** etc.: exposed to the full force of accident, even in accident's very path. 32. **jump with:** agree with. 34. **to thee:** let me approach THEE. 37. **go about:** undertake. 41. **estates:** rank and position.

Were purchas'd by the merit of the wearer!
How many then should cover that stand bare!
How many be commanded that command!   45
How much low peasantry would then be gleaned
From the true seed of honor! and how much honor
Pick'd from the chaff and ruin of the times
To be new varnish'd! Well, but to my choice.
"Who chooseth me shall get as much as he deserves."   50
I will assume desert. Give me a key for this,
And instantly unlock my fortunes here. [*He opens the silver casket.*]

POR.   [*aside*] Too long a pause for that which you find there.

ARR.   What's here? The portrait of a blinking idiot,
Presenting me a schedule! I will read it.   55
How much unlike art thou to Portia!
How much unlike my hopes and my deservings!
"Who chooseth me shall have as much as he deserves."
Did I deserve no more than a fool's head?
Is that my prize? Are my deserts no better?   60

POR.   To offend and judge are distinct offices
And of opposed natures.

ARR.   What is here?
"The fire seven times tried this.
Seven times tried that judgment is
That did never choose amiss.   65
Some there be that shadows kiss;
Such have but a shadow's bliss.
There be fools alive iwis
Silver'd o'er, and so was this.
Take what wife you will to bed,   70
I will ever be your head.
So be gone; you are sped."
Still more fool I shall appear
By the time I linger here.

---

43. **purchas'd:** won. The emphatic word is *merit*. 44. **should cover:** would put on their hats. 46. **peasantry:** persons whose character befits a low rank. 47. **the true seed of honor:** the genuine children of honor, the true and proper nobility. 49. **to my choice:** let me concentrate on choosing. 51. **assume.** Emphatic, "I will take it for granted that I deserve success." *This* is also emphatic. 55. **schedule!** scroll. 61. **To offend and judge,** etc.: the offender should remember that his position is not that of judge. Portia says this because the Prince, though he has committed a fault by choosing wrong, is presuming to blame his misery on the terms of the wager. 63. **fire.** dissyllabic (as if *fi-er*).—**this:** i.e., this silver. 68. **iwis.** An old adjective or adverb meaning "certainly." It was obsolete in Shakespeare's time, except in poetry, and was frequently taken as if it were the pronoun *I* and a verb *wis,* "know." 71. **I will ever be your head:** i.e., you will always have a fool's head, always be a fool. 72. **you are sped:** your fortune is made—an ironical idiom equivalent to "your case is settled." 74. **By the time,** etc.: i.e., the longer I linger here, the bigger fool I shall seem.

	With one fool's head I came to woo,	75

With one fool's head I came to woo, 75
But I go away with two.
Sweet, adieu. I'll keep my oath,
Patiently to bear my wroth.   [*Exit with his Train.*]

POR.   Thus hath the candle sing'd the moth.
O, these deliberate fools! When they do choose,   80
They have the wisdom by their wit to lose.

NER.   The ancient saying is no heresy,
Hanging and wiving goes by destiny.

POR.   Come draw the curtain, Nerissa.

Enter Messenger.

MESS.   Where is my lady?

POR.   Here. What would my lord?   85

MESS.   Madam, there is alighted at your gate
A young Venetian, one that comes before
To signify th' approaching of his lord;
From whom he bringeth sensible regreets,
To wit, besides commends and courteous breath,   90
Gifts of rich value. Yet I have not seen
So likely an ambassador of love.
A day in April never came so sweet
To show how costly summer was at hand
As this fore-spurrer comes before his lord.   95

POR.   No more, I pray thee. I am half afeard
Thou wilt say anon he is some kin to thee,
Thou spend'st such high-day wit in praising him.
Come, come, Nerissa; for I long to see
Quick Cupid's post that comes so mannerly.   100

NER.   Bassanio, Lord Love, if thy will it be!   *Exeunt.*

---

78. **wroth:** vexatious lot, discomfiture. 81. **They have the wisdom,** etc.: They are so wise that, when they have used all their wisdom in deliberating, they choose wrong, and lose. 83. **Hanging...destiny.** Marriage and hanging both occur by fate —**goes.** Note singular verb. 85. **my lord.** Said jestingly, of course; Portia is light-headed at her escape from another unwelcome suitor. 89. **sensible regreets:** greetings that show his deep feeling. 90. **commends:** regards, expressions of devotion. 92. **likely:** promising, attractive. 94. **costly:** rich, bountiful. 98. **high-day wit:** cleverness that befits the eloquence appropriate to a festival. 101. **Lord Love.** Nerissa addresses her prayer to the god of love, a fresh reminder of Portia's affections.

ACT III

SCENE I. [*Venice. A street.*]

Enter Solanio *and* Salerio.

SOLAN.	Now what news on the Rialto?
SALER.	Why, yet it lives there uncheck'd that Antonio hath a ship of rich lading wrack'd on the narrow seas—the Goodwins I think they call the place—a very dangerous flat, and fatal, where the carcases of many a tall ship lie buried, as they say, if my gossip Report be an honest woman of her word. 6
SOLAN.	I would she were as lying a gossip in that as ever knapp'd ginger or made her neighbours believe she wept for the death of a third husband. But it is true, without any slips of prolixity or crossing the plain highway of talk, that the good Antonio, the honest Antonio—O that I had a title good enough to keep his name company!— 11
SALER.	Come, the full stop.
SOLAN.	Ha, what sayest thou? Why, the end is, he hath lost a ship.
SALER.	I would it might prove the end of his losses.
SOLAN.	Let me say amen betimes, lest the devil cross my prayer, for here he comes in the likeness of a Jew. 16

Enter Shylock.

	How now, Shylock? What news among the merchants?
SHY.	You knew, none so well, none so well as you, of my daughter's flight.
SALER.	That's certain. I, for my part, knew the tailor that made the wings she flew withal. *proud* 20
SOLAN.	And Shylock, for his own part, knew the bird was fledge; and then it is the complexion of them all to leave the dam.

ACT III. SCENE I.
2. **it lives there uncheck'd:** the report circulates without contradiction. 3. **the Goodwins:** the Goodwin Sands, a dangerous shoal in the English Channel. 5. **tall:** gallant.—**gossip:** old acquaintance—with a suggestion of the modern meaning of *gossip*. 7. **knapp'd:** bit off. Old people carried ginger root and similar things in their pockets or pouches to nibble at. 9-10. **slips of prolixity:** wordy lies. A *slip* was a "counterfeit coin."—**crossing the plain highway of talk:** violating the plain truth of language. Almost as great a jabberer as Gratiano, Solanio means that the report is the mere truth. 10. **honest:** honorable. 12. **the full stop:** i.e., put a period to your report, tell us the truth and have done. 15. **betimes:** in good season, quickly. 19-20. **knew the tailor,** etc.: i.e., knew the person who contrived her flight. There may be an allusion to the fact that Jessica's disguise (boy's clothes) assisted her to escape.—**withal:** with. 21-22. **was fledge:** i.e., was old enough to run away.—**complexion:** temperament, disposition (though sometimes it means the color of skin).

SHY.	She is damn'd for it.
SALER.	That's certain, if the devil may be her judge.
SHY.	My own flesh and blood to rebel! 25
SOLAN.	Out upon it, old carrion! Rebels it at these years?
SHY.	I say my daughter is my flesh and my blood.
SALER.	There is more difference between thy flesh and hers than between jet and ivory; more between your bloods than there is between red wine and Rhenish. But tell us, do you hear whether Antonio have had any loss at sea or no?[†] 31
SHY.	There I have another bad match! A bankrout, a prodigal, who dare scarce show his head on the Rialto! a beggar, that was us'd to come so smug upon the mart! Let him look to his bond. He was wont to call me usurer. Let him look to his bond. He was wont to lend money for a Christian cursy. Let him look to his bond. 36
SALER.	Why, I am sure, if he forfeit, thou wilt not take his flesh. What's that good for?
SHY.	To bait fish withal. If it will feed nothing else, it will feed my revenge. He hath disgrac'd me, and hind'red me half a million; laugh'd at my losses, mock'd at my gains, scorned my nation, thwarted my bargains, cooled my friends, heated mine enemies—and what's his reason? I am a Jew. Hath not a Jew eyes? Hath not a Jew hands, organs, dimensions, senses, affections, passions? fed with the same food, hurt with the same weapons, subject to the same diseases, healed by the same means, warmed and cooled by the same winter and summer as a Christian is? If you prick us, do we not bleed? If you tickle us, do we not laugh? If you poison us, do we not die? And if you wrong us, shall we not revenge? If we are like you in the rest, we will resemble you in that. If a Jew wrong a Christian, what is his humility? Revenge. If a Christian wrong a Jew, what should his sufferance be by Christian example?

---

24. **the devil.** *Devil* is emphatic. Salerio means that no good man can blame her for running away. He also insinuates that the Jew and the devil are one (cf. line 15, above). 26. **Out upon it:** curses upon it.—**Rebels it,** etc. Solanio chooses to misunderstand Shylock, as if he had spoken of his own passions as unruly. *Blood* often means "passions" or "impulses." 32. **bad match!** bad bargain. Shylock's first bad match was the falling out with Jessica. 34. **smug:** trim, finely dressed. 36. **for a Christian cursy:** as an act of politeness between Christians. 39. **withal:** with. 40. **He hath disgrac'd me,** etc. Shylock makes Antonio a scapegoat for all the insults and injuries which the money lender has endured from the Christians. 43-44. **dimensions:** members.—**affections:** feelings. 50. **what is his humility?** What kind of Christian humility does he show?

---

†   The non-verbal gestures of Salerio and Salerno in the BBC version as they mock, torment, and even tickle the Jew intensify the cruelty of the scene, so that Shylock's humiliation becomes unbearable. [K.R.]

Why, revenge. The villainy you teach me I will execute, and it shall go
hard but I will better the instruction. *tables turned*   53

Enter a Man *from Antonio.*

MAN.   Gentlemen, my master Antonio is at his house, and desires to speak
        with you both.

SALER. We have been up and down to seek him.

Enter Tubal.

SOLAN. Here comes another of the tribe. A third cannot be match'd, unless the
        devil himself turn Jew.   *Exeunt* [*Solanio, Salerio, and Man*].

SHY.   How now, Tubal? What news from Genoa? Hast thou found my
        daughter?   60

TUB.   I often came where I did hear of her, but cannot find her.

SHY.   Why, there, there, there, there! A diamond gone cost me two thousand
        ducats in Frankford! The curse never fell upon our nation till now; I
        never felt it till now. Two thousand ducats in that, and other precious,
        precious jewels. I would my daughter were dead at my foot, and the
        jewels in her ear! Would she were hears'd at my foot, and the ducats in
        her coffin! No news of them? Why, so—and I know not what's spent
        in the search. Why, thou loss upon loss! the thief gone with so much,
        and so much to find the thief; and no satisfaction, no revenge! nor no
        ill luck stirring but what lights o' my shoulders; no sighs but o' my
        breathing; no tears but o' my shedding.   71

TUB.   Yes, other men have ill luck too.
        Antonio, as I heard in Genoa—

SHY.   What, what, what? Ill luck, ill luck?

TUB.   Hath an argosy cast away coming from Tripolis.   75

SHY.   I thank God, I thank God! Is it true? is it true?

TUB.   I spoke with some of the sailors that escaped the wrack.

SHY.   I thank thee, good Tubal. Good news, good news! Ha, ha! Where? in
        Genoa?

TUB.   Your daughter spent in Genoa, as I heard, one night fourscore ducats.

SHY.   Thou stick'st a dagger in me. I shall never see my gold again. Fourscore
        ducats at a sitting! fourscore ducats!   82

52-53. **it shall go hard but I will better the instruction:** I will go to any trouble to improve what the
Christians have taught me about revenge. *But* means "unless." *It shall go hard* is an idiomatic expression
of assurance, implying that the speaker will make every effort to bring about what he declares. 62. **A
diamond gone cost me:** i.e., which cost me.

TUB.   There came divers of Antonio's creditors in my company to Venice that
           swear he cannot choose but break.   84

SHY.   I am very glad of it. I'll plague him; I'll torture him. I am glad of it.

TUB.   One of them showed me a ring that he had of your daughter for a
           monkey.

SHY.   Out upon her! Thou torturest me, Tubal. It was my turquoise; I had
           it of Leah when I was a bachelor. I would not have given it for a
           wilderness of monkeys.†   90

TUB.   But Antonio is certainly undone.

SHY.   Nay, that's true, that's very true. Go, Tubal, fee me an officer; bespeak
           him a fortnight before. I will have the heart of him if he forfeit; for,
           were he out of Venice, I can make what merchandise I will. Go, Tubal,
           and meet me at our synagogue; go, good Tubal; at our synagogue,
           Tubal.   *Exeunt.* 96

SCENE II. [*Belmont. Portia's house.*]

Enter Bassanio, Portia, Gratiano, *and all their Trains;* [Nerissa].

POR.   I pray you tarry; pause a day or two
           Before you hazard; for in choosing wrong
           I lose your company. Therefore forbear awhile.
           There's something tells me (but it is not love)
           I would not lose you; and you know yourself   5

---

84. **he cannot choose but break:** he cannot help becoming a bankrupt. 87. This brief utterance by Tubal about the fate of the turquoise ring (traded for a monkey) that was given to Shylock by his beloved Leah captures in a few words the central importance of the "ring" plot to the entire play. [K.R.] 89. **Leah:** Shylock's wife. Jessica's sale of the ring that Leah gave Shylock breaks his heart, and reveals his softer side 92. **an officer.** A sheriff's officer, to make the arrest.—**bespeak him:** engage him. 94. **I can make what merchandise I will:** I can drive as hard bargains as I wish. Though Shylock speaks of merchandise, he may be thinking principally of bargains in the way of money-lending, which Antonio subverts by making interest free loans.

---

†   Tubal's news from Genoa that Jessica has squandered four-score ducats in one night comes as a devastating shock to miserly Shylock but, even worse, it turns out that she has bartered away a turquoise ring for a monkey. It is the ring that Shylock's beloved Leah had given him. Michael Radford uses this single line to invent an intriguing subplot about Jessica's betrayal of her father. At the end of the film, a close-up shows the ring still on Jessica's finger, which makes it apparent that she may never have committed this dreadful deed. Radford opens up a possibility that the information from Genoa was idle gossip, even though nowhere else in the play is there support for such a theory. [K.R.]

Hate counsels not in such a quality.
But lest you should not understand me well—
And yet a maiden hath no tongue but thought—
I would detain you here some month or two
Before you venture for me. I could teach you   10
How to choose right, but then I am forsworn.
So will I never be; so may you miss me;
But if you do, you'll make me wish a sin—
That I had been forsworn. Beshrow your eyes!
They have o'erlook'd me and divided me;   15
One half of me is yours, the other half yours—
Mine own, I would say; but if mine, then yours,
And so all yours! O, these naughty times
Puts bars between the owners and their rights!
And so, though yours, not yours. Prove it so,   20
Let fortune go to hell for it, not I.
I speak too long; but 'tis to peize the time,
To eche it, and to draw it out in length,
To stay you from election.

Bass.   Let me choose;
For as I am, I live upon the rack.   25

Por.   Upon the rack, Bassanio? Then confess
What treason there is mingled with your love.

Bass.   None but that ugly treason of mistrust,
Which makes me fear th' enjoying of my love.
There may as well be amity and life   30
'Tween snow and fire as treason and my love.

Por.   Ay, but I fear you speak upon the rack,
Where men enforced do speak anything.

Bass.   Promise me life, and I'll confess the truth.

Por.   Well then, confess and live.

Scene II.
6. **Hate counsels not in such a quality.** *Hate* is the emphatic word. Feelings of hatred would not generate such a quality of kindly advice as this. 14. **Beshrow:** literally, "curse" always used lightly or (as here) tenderly. 15. **o'erlook'd me:** bewitched me. 18. **naughty:** bad. The word then directed at adults was not trivial as it is now. 20. **Prove it so:** if it should turn out to be that I am not to be yours. 21. **Let fortune,** etc.: i.e., let fortune, not I, be condemned for it 22. **peize.** Literally, "to weigh"; here, "to add to." 23. **eche:** to lengthen The same idea as expressed above in line 22. 24. **To stay you from election:** to delay your choosing. 27. **What treason,** etc. Said mischievously. The torture of the rack was used to extract confessions from the guilty. Since he is "on the rack" Portia jestingly suggests that he confess any falsehood that may be mingled with his affection. 33. **enforced:** under compulsion. The dialogue is carried out in the same jesting vein about the rack Portia began with.

BASS.   "Confess" and "love"   35
          Had been the very sum of my confession.
          O happy torment, when my torturer
          Doth teach me answers for deliverance!
          But let me to my fortune and the caskets.

POR.   Away then! I am lock'd in one of them.†   40
          If you do love me, you will find me out.
          Nerissa and the rest, stand all aloof.
          Let music sound while he doth make his choice;
          Then, if he lose, he makes a swanlike end,
          Fading in music. That the comparison   45
          May stand more proper, my eye shall be the stream
          And wat'ry deathbed for him. He may win;
          And what is music then? Then music is
          Even as the flourish when true subjects bow
          To a new-crowned monarch. Such it is   50
          As are those dulcet sounds in break of day
          That creep into the dreaming bridegroom's ear
          And summon him to marriage. Now he goes
          With no less presence, but with much more love,
          Than young Alcides when he did redeem   55
          The virgin tribute paid by howling Troy
          To the sea monster. I stand for sacrifice;
          The rest aloof are the Dardanian wives,
          With bleared visages come forth to view
          The issue of th' exploit. Go, Hercules!   60
          Live thou, I live. With much much more dismay
          I view the fight than thou that mak'st the fray.

          A Song, the whilst Bassanio *comments on the caskets to himself.*

---

41. **If you do love me, you will find me out.** There is an implication that Portia's father believed that the caskets would make a proper choice for his daughter. 45. **Fading in music.** The "swan song," the belief that swans sing at the point of death. George Orwell's famous mixed metaphor, poking fun at bad lefty writing, comes to mind: "The fascist octopus sings his swan song." [K.R.] 46. **May stand more proper:** may be more appropriate. —**my eye shall be the stream,** etc.: i.e., if he chooses wrong I will drown him with my tears. 49. **flourish:** flourish of trumpets. 54. **With no less presence:** with as fine an appearance and bearing. 55. **Alcides:** Hercules.—**redeem:** rescue. 56. **The virgin tribute paid by howling Troy:** i.e., by the lamenting Trojans. 57. **I stand for sacrifice:** I stand here in place of the maiden about to be sacrificed. 58. **Dardanian:** Trojan. 61. **Live thou:** i.e., if thou live.

---

† For Portia the suspense could never be more unbearable than during the moments when Bassanio himself takes on the challenge of choosing the casket. The famous song, with the ubiquitous rhymes on "lead," is belted out in the Olivier version by a duet of geriatric choristers, while Derbhle Crotty as Portia in the Nunn TV film turns Bassanio's choice of a casket into a quasi-religious rite. She prays stiff-backed on a kneeler and even crosses herself. Faithful Nerissa competently handles the solo role of chorister. [K.R.]

Portia (Derbhle Crotty) steels herself for the outcome of Bassanio's (Alexander Hanson) search for the right casket. (Nunn, 2001)

sung:

> Tell me, where is fancy bred,— *clue?*
> Or in the heart, or in the head?
> How begot, how nourished?   65
>   Reply, reply.
> It is engend'red in the eyes,
> With gazing fed; and fancy dies *—clue?*
> In the cradle where it lies.
>   Let us all ring fancy's knell.   70
>   I'll begin it—Ding, dong, bell.

ALL.   Ding, dong, bell.

BASS.   So may the outward shows be least themselves; *— he would know*
         The world is still deceiv'd with ornament.
         In law, what plea so tainted and corrupt   75
         But, being season'd with a gracious voice,
         Obscures the show of evil? In religion,
         What damned error but some sober brow
         Will bless it, and approve it with a text,

---

63. **fancy:** love.—As Bassanio deliberates over the choice of caskets, this song that builds its rhymes around "lead" fills the air. Whether or not it is deliberately devised as a hint to Bassanio raises serious question about Portia's integrity in conforming to her father's wishes, and/or the possibility that her declarations of faith to him are mere hypocrisy. [K.R.] 73. **So may the outward shows be least themselves.** Bassanio is looking at the caskets. Outward appearance may not coincide with reality—a favorite Shakespearean theme. For full definition, see 3.2.97-98, below. 74. **still:** ever. 77. **Obscures the show of evil:** a smooth talker with a pleasant or elegant voice covers up evil action. 79. **approve:** prove, demonstrate.

Hiding the grossness with fair ornament?   80
There is no vice so simple but assumes
Some mark of virtue on his outward parts.
How many cowards, whose hearts are all as false
As stairs of sand, wear yet upon their chins
The beards of Hercules and frowning Mars;   85
Who, inward search'd, have livers white as milk!
And these assume but valour's excrement
To render them redoubted. Look on beauty,
And you shall see 'tis purchas'd by the weight,
Which therein works a miracle in nature,   90
Making them lightest that wear most of it.
So are those crisped snaky golden locks
Which make such wanton gambols with the wind   *deciedes not to*
Upon supposed fairness often known   *go with beauty*
To be the dowry of a second head,   95
The skull that bred them in the sepulchre.
Thus ornament is but the guiled shore
To a most dangerous sea; the beauteous scarf
Veiling an Indian beauty; in a word,
The seeming truth which cunning times put on   100
To entrap the wisest. Therefore, thou gaudy gold,
Hard food for Midas, I will none of thee;
Nor none of thee, thou pale and common drudge   *pour*
'Tween man and man: but thou, thou meagre lead,
Which rather threaten'st than dost promise aught,   105
Thy plainness moves me more than eloquence;
And here choose I. Joy be the consequence!

POR.   [aside] How all the other passions fleet to air,
As doubtful thoughts, and rash-embrac'd despair,
And shudd'ring fear, and green-ey'd jealousy!   110
O love, be moderate; allay thy ecstasy;

---

86. **livers white as milk.** Cowards were supposed to have white livers. Cf. *white-livered,* "thou lily-liver'd boy" (*Macbeth,* 5. 3). 87. **excrement:** outgrowth. Here used of the beard, sometimes used also of the nails. 88. **redoubted:** feared, dreaded. 91. **lightest.** With a pun on *light* in the sense of "unchaste." 93. **wanton:** sportive. 95. **dowry:** possession. The Elizabethan dramatists abound in satirical references to the practice of wearing false hair. 97. **guiled:** guile, deceptive. 99. **an Indian beauty.** *Indian* is of course emphatic. What is meant is a black beauty, a concept Elizabethans might have trouble with since they idealized fair women, a notable exception being Shakespeare's sonnet #130. 102. **Hard food for Midas:** Midas loved gold but his favorite metal was regrettably inedible. 103, 104. **thou pale and common drudge 'Tween man and man:** silver, which was the ordinary currency in Shakespeare's time. 104. **meagre:** poor,—as being valueless in comparison with silver and gold. 110. **green-ey'd jealousy!** Shakespeare calls jealousy the "green-ey'd monster'" in *Othello,* 3.3, where the Moor is speaking of it under the figure of a green-eyed tiger, or some other savage animal. It was supposed that suspicious people suffering from a disease of the bile, called jaundice, often have greenish-yellow eyes.

In measure rain thy joy; scant this excess!
I feel too much thy blessing. Make it less
For fear I surfeit!

BASS.   [*opening the leaden casket*] What find I here?
Fair Portia's counterfeit! What demigod   115
Hath come so near creation? Move these eyes?
Or whether, riding on the balls of mine,
Seem they in motion? Here are sever'd lips,
Parted with sugar breath. So sweet a bar
Should sunder such sweet friends. Here in her hairs   120
The painter plays the spider; and hath woven
A golden mesh t' entrap the hearts of men
Faster than gnats in cobwebs. But her eyes—
How could he see to do them? Having made one,
Methinks it should have power to steal both his   125
And leave itself unfurnish'd. Yet look, how far
The substance of my praise doth wrong this shadow
In underprizing it, so far this shadow
Doth limp behind the substance. Here's the scroll,
The continent and summary of my fortune.   130
"You that choose not by the view
Chance as fair and choose as true.
Since this fortune falls to you,
Be content and seek no new.
If you be well pleas'd with this   135
And hold your fortune for your bliss,
Turn you where your lady is
And claim her with a loving kiss."
A gentle scroll. Fair lady, by your leave;   [*Kisses her.*]
I come by note, to give and to receive.   140
Like one of two contending in a prize,
That thinks he hath done well in people's eyes,
Hearing applause and universal shout,

---

114. **For fear I surfeit!** for fear that I become sick from having too much. 115-16. **counterfeit:** portrait—**What demigod Hath come so near creation?** i.e., the painter has come so near to life that he must be at least a demigod. 119. **So sweet a bar,** etc.: i.e., Only a bar, so sweet as this, should sunder such sweet friends. 126. **And leave itself unfurnish'd:** i.e., The imagery here becomes sufficiently intricate almost to qualify as "metaphysical" after the manner of John Donne [K.R.]. By stealing away both the painter's eyes, the single eye that he had painted would need to remain alone without its mate, for a blind painter could not complete the picture. 129. **the substance:** the reality, i.e., Portia herself. 130. **The continent:** that which contains—hence practically equivalent to "summary." 132. **Chance as fair and choose as true:** A plucky gamble will lead you to the right choice. 136. **hold your fortune for your bliss:** regard what has happened to you as your great happiness in life. 140. **by note:** in accordance with the directions of his scroll. 141: **a prize:** a contest for a prize.

Giddy in spirit, still gazing in a doubt
Whether those peals of praise be his or no;   145
So, thrice-fair lady, stand I, even so,
As doubtful whether what I see be true,
Until confirm'd, sign'd, ratified by you.

POR.   You see me, Lord Bassanio, where I stand,
Such as I am. Though for myself alone   150
I would not be ambitious in my wish
To wish myself much better, yet for you
I would be trebled twenty times myself,
A thousand times more fair, ten thousand times more rich,
That, only to stand high in your account,   155
I might in virtues, beauties, livings, friends,
Exceed account. But the full sum of me
Is sum of nothing, which, to term in gross,
Is an unlesson'd girl, unschool'd, unpractis'd;
Happy in this, she is not yet so old   160
But she may learn; happier than this,
She is not bred so dull but she can learn;
Happiest of all is that her gentle spirit
Commits itself to yours to be directed,
As from her lord, her governor, her king.   165
Myself and what is mine to you and yours
Is now converted. But now I was the lord
Of this fair mansion, master of my servants,
Queen o'er myself; and even now, but now,
This house, these servants, and this same myself   170
Are yours, my lord's. I give them with this ring;   *material importance of ring*
Which when you part from, lose, or give away,
Let it presage the ruin of your love
And be my vantage to exclaim on you.

---

147. **what I see:** the portrait and the scroll, which indicate that he has won. 140-150: In its formality this set speech of Bassanio begins to sound like an epic simile [K.R.]. 157. **Exceed account:** exceed computation. 157–160. **the full sum,** etc.: when all that I am is summed up in full it amounts only to something which must be described as, etc.—**to term in gross:** to mention at its full amount. I am something which must be termed only, etc. The Folios have "sum of nothing." This would mean "when all that I am is summed up, it is the same as if one summed up nothing." The Quarto reading is [perhaps]better: "when I am summed up, it is as if one summed up something which amounted, when computed in gross, to merely an unlesson'd girl," The entire hyperbolic [inflated] speech is untypical of Portia's usual self-assurance and reminiscent of Kate's speech of submission at the close of *The Taming of the Shrew* [K.R.]. 165. **from.** As if she had said "to receive directions" instead of "to be directed." 166-67. **Myself...converted:** *I* am now changed to *you,* and *mine* is changed to *yours.* 174. **be my vantage to exclaim on you:** If you lose, etc., this ring, let that loss be regarded as my opportunity to cry out against you!

Bass.	Madam, you have bereft me of all words,
	Only my blood speaks to you in my veins;
	And there is such confusion in my powers
	As, after some oration fairly spoke
	By a beloved prince, there doth appear
	Among the buzzing pleased multitude,
	Where every something, being blent together,
	Turns to a wild of nothing, save of joy,
	Express'd and not express'd. But when this ring
	Parts from this finger, then parts life from hence!
	O, then be bold to say Bassanio's dead!
Ner.	My lord and lady, it is now our time
	That have stood by and seen our wishes prosper
	To cry "good joy." Good joy, my lord and lady!
Gra.	My Lord Bassanio, and my gentle lady,
	I wish you all the joy that you can wish;
	For I am sure you can wish none from me;
	And when your honors mean to solemnize
	The bargain of your faith, I do beseech you
	Even at that time I may be married too.
Bass.	With all my heart, so thou canst get a wife.
Gra.	I thank your lordship, you have got me one.
	My eyes, my lord, can look as swift as yours.
	You saw the mistress, I beheld the maid;
	You lov'd, I lov'd; for intermission
	No more pertains to me, my lord, than you.
	Your fortune stood upon the caskets there,
	And so did mine too, as the matter falls;
	For wooing here until I sweat again,
	And swearing till my very roof was dry
	With oaths of love, at last—if promise last—
	I got a promise of this fair one here Nerissa
	To have her love, provided that your fortune
	Achiev'd her mistress.
Por.	Is this true, Nerissa?

Line numbers: 175, 180, 185, 190, 195, 200, 205

182. **a wild of nothing:** a chaos wherein nothing is discernible. 184. **from hence!** Probably with a gesture, his hand on his heart. 191. **you can wish none from me:** i.e., "you cannot need my good wishes." Hence he says he wishes them all the joy that *they* can wish themselves. *You* is emphatic. 195. **so:** provided that.—**thou.** Bassanio uses *thou* to Gratiano as to an inferior; Gratiano addresses him with the respectful *you.* 199. **for intermission:** to occupy the leisure time that your devotion allowed me. 200. **No more,** etc.: i.e., my success in love was no more due to my own efforts than your success was to yours; in both cases we have the caskets to thank. 205. **if promise last:** if her promise hold good. 208. **Achiev'd:** won.

NER.	Madam, it is, so you stand pleas'd withal.	
BASS.	And do you, Gratiano, mean good faith?	210
GRA.	Yes, faith, my lord.	
BASS.	Our feast shall be much honored in your marriage.	
GRA.	We'll play with them the first boy for a thousand ducats.	
NER.	What, and stake down?	
GRA.	No, we shall ne'er win at that sport, and stake down.	215

GRA. But who comes here? Lorenzo and his infidel?
What, and my old Venetian friend Salerio?

Enter Lorenzo, Jessica, *and* Salerio *(a Messenger from Venice).*

BASS. Lorenzo and Salerio, welcome hither,
If that the youth of my new int'rest here
Have power to bid you welcome. By your leave,   220
I bid my very friends and countrymen,
Sweet Portia, welcome.

POR.   So do I, my lord.
They are entirely welcome.

LOR. I thank your honor. For my part, my lord,
My purpose was not to have seen you here;   225
But meeting with Salerio by the way,
He did entreat me, past all saying nay,
To come with him along.

SALER.   I did, my lord,
And I have reason for it. Signior Antonio
Commends him to you.   [*Gives Bassanio a letter.*]

BASS.   Ere I ope his letter,   230
I pray you tell me how my good friend doth.

SALER. Not sick, my lord, unless it be in mind;
Nor well, unless in mind. His letter there
Will show you his estate. Open the letter.

GRA. Nerissa, cheer yond stranger; bid her welcome.   235

---

209. **so you stand pleas'd withal:** provided you are pleased with it. *Stand* often means little more than be. 213. **We'll play...ducats:** "We'll bet on which couple has a son first." [K.R.] 216. **stake down:** lay down the stakes—with a pun. 218. **his infidel:** i.e., Jessica, so called because she is a Jewess. 219. **If that:** if.—**the youth of my new int'rest here:** the fact that it is only a short time since I have had any claim to command in this household. Bassanio refers to the fact that he had only recently, by virtue of his betrothal to Portia, any right to act as host. 221. **my very friends:** my true friends. 225. **to have seen.** The perfect infinitive is common after verbs of wishing. 230. **Commends him to you:** sends you his regards. 234. **his estate:** his state, his condition.

Your hand, Salerio. What's the news from Venice?
How doth that royal merchant, good Antonio?
I know he will be glad of our success.
We are the Jasons, we have won the Fleece. *reference to act I*

SALER.   I would you had won the fleece that he hath lost!   240

POR.   There are some shrowd contents in yond same paper
That steals the colour from Bassanio's cheek:
Some dear friend dead; else nothing in the world
Could turn so much the constitution
Of any constant man. What, worse and worse?   245
With leave, Bassanio—I am half yourself,
And I must freely have the half of anything
That this same paper brings you.

BASS.   O sweet Portia,
Here are a few of the unpleasant'st words
That ever blotted paper! Gentle lady,   250
When I did first impart my love to you,
I freely told you all the wealth I had
Ran in my veins—I was a gentleman;
And then I told you true; and yet, dear lady,
Rating myself at nothing, you shall see   255
How much I was a braggart. When I told you
My state was nothing, I should then have told you
That I was worse than nothing; for indeed
I have engag'd myself to a dear friend, ✗
Engag'd my friend to his mere enemy   260
To feed my means. Here is a letter, lady—
The paper as the body of my friend,
And every word in it a gaping wound
Issuing lifeblood. But is it true, Salerio?
Have all his ventures fail'd? What, not one hit?   265
From Tripolis, from Mexico, and England,
From Lisbon, Barbary, and India?
And not one vessel scape the dreadful touch
Of merchant-marring rocks?

---

239. **the Fleece:** in Greek mythology Jason slew a dragon to obtain the golden fleece and regain his throne. [K.R.] 240. **he:** i.e., Antonio. 241. **shrowd.** Literally, "cursed," and so "bad." 244-45. **constitution... constant.** The alliteration is doubtless intentional. *Constant* means "collected," "firm in temper," "self-contained," etc. 245. **What, worse and worse?** Portia notices that the letter is making Bassanio look more and more disturbed 246. **With leave:** by your leave. 252. **I freely told you.** Although Bassanio is sometimes described as a fortune-hunter, here he does not conceal his poverty 260. **mere enemy:** his utter, out-and-out enemy. 262. **The paper as,** etc.: the paper is, as it were, etc. 269. **merchant-marring.** *Merchant* often means "merchantmen," "merchant vessel," as in this compound.

SALER.   Not one, my lord.
        Besides, it should appear that, if he had   270
        The present money to discharge the Jew,
        He would not take it. Never did I know
        A creature that did bear the shape of man
        So keen and greedy to confound a man.
        He plies the Duke at morning and at night,   275
        And doth impeach the freedom of the state
        If they deny him justice. Twenty merchants,
        The Duke himself, and the magnificoes
        Of greatest port have all persuaded with him;
        But none can drive him from the envious plea   280
        Of forfeiture, of justice, and his bond.

JES.   When I was with him, I have heard him swear
        To Tubal and to Chus, his countrymen,
        That he would rather have Antonio's flesh
        Than twenty times the value of the sum   285
        That he did owe him; and I know, my lord,
        If law, authority, and power deny not,
        It will go hard with poor Antonio.

POR.   Is it your dear friend that is thus in trouble?

BASS.   The dearest friend to me, the kindest man,   290
        The best-condition'd and unwearied spirit
        In doing courtesies, and one in whom
        The ancient Roman honor more appears — like portia's compliments
        Than any that draws breath in Italy.

POR.   What sum owes he the Jew?   295

BASS.   For me three thousand ducats.

POR.   What, no more?
        Pay him six thousand, and deface the bond.
        Double six thousand and then treble that
        Before a friend of this description
        Shall lose a hair through Bassanio's fault.   300
        First go with me to church and call me wife, first her, second Antonio

---

274. **confound:** ruin, destroy. The repetition of *man* is intentional. 276. **Doth impeach the freedom of the state:** accuses the state of not being a free state, i.e., of not guaranteeing the rights of its citizens. 278. **magnificoes:** great nobles. 279. **Of greatest port:** the greatest dignity. *Port* literally means "bearing," "demeanour." 280. **envious:** malignant. 281. **Of forfeiture, of justice, and his bond.** These are key words, which Shylock uses in his suit to the Duke, preparing the way for his reiteration of them later in the trial scene. 289. **your dear friend:** i.e., the true friend that you mentioned just now (see line 259). 291. **best-condition'd:** furnished with or characterized by the best conditions, i.e., characteristics, traits.—**spirit.** Often used of persons, as here. 297. **deface:** destroy.

And then away to Venice to your friend!
For never shall you lie by Portia's side
With an unquiet soul. You shall have gold
To pay the petty debt twenty times over.   305
When it is paid, bring your true friend along.
My maid Nerissa and myself meantime
Will live as maids and widows. Come, away!
For you shall hence upon your wedding day.
Bid your friends welcome, show a merry cheer;   310
Since you are dear bought, I will love you dear.   *remember for*
But let me hear the letter of your friend.   *flesh bond in act 4*

BASS. "Sweet Bassanio, my ships have all miscarried, my creditors grow
cruel, my estate is very low, my bond to the Jew is forfeit; and since in
paying it, it is impossible I should live, all debts are clear'd between you
and I if I might but see you at my death. Notwithstanding, use your
pleasure. If your love do not persuade you to come, let not my letter."

POR. O love, dispatch all business and be gone! *she understands*   318

BASS. Since I have your good leave to go away,
I will make haste; but till I come again,   320
No bed shall e'er be guilty of my stay,
Nor rest be interposer 'twixt us twain.   *Exeunt.*

SCENE III. [*Venice. The street before Shylock's house.*]

Enter [Shylock] *the Jew and* Solanio *and* Antonio *and the* Jailer.

SHY. Jailer, look to him. Tell not me of mercy.
This is the fool that lent out money gratis.
Jailer, look to him.

ANT.   Hear me yet, good Shylock.

SHY. I'll have my bond! Speak not against my bond!
I have sworn an oath that I will have my bond.   5
Thou call'dst me dog before thou hadst a cause;
But, since I am a dog, beware my fangs.
The Duke shall grant me justice. I do wonder,

---

308. **as maids and widows:** i.e., "as maidens who have lost their lovers." "Though unmarried, we shall
lament your absence as widows lament the loss of their husbands." 311. **Since you are dear bought.**
Referring to the danger of Antonio. Portia has secured Bassanio, but only at the price of Antonio's
deadly peril. 313. **have all miscarried:** have all been lost. 321. **No bed shall e'er be guilty of my stay.**
Bassanio takes an oath which is common in old romances,—not to sleep until he has accomplished his
undertaking.

	Thou naughty jailer, that thou art so fond	
	To come abroad with him at his request.	10
ANT.	I pray thee hear me speak.	
SHY.	I'll have my bond. I will not hear thee speak.	
	I'll have my bond, and therefore speak no more.	
	I'll not be made a soft and dull-ey'd fool,	
	To shake the head, relent, and sigh, and yield	15
	To Christian intercessors. Follow not.	
	I'll have no speaking; I will have my bond.	*Exit.*
SOLAN.	It is the most impenetrable cur	
	That ever kept with men.	
ANT.	Let him alone.	
	I'll follow him no more with bootless prayers.	20
	He seeks my life. His reason well I know:	
	I oft deliver'd from his forfeitures	
	Many that have at times made moan to me.	
	Therefore he hates me.	
SOLAN.	I am sure the Duke	
	Will never grant this forfeiture to hold.	25
ANT.	The Duke cannot deny the course of law;	
	For the commodity that strangers have	
	With us in Venice, if it be denied,	
	Will much impeach the justice of the state,	
	Since that the trade and profit of the city	30
	Consisteth of all nations. Therefore go.	
	These griefs and losses have so bated me	
	That I shall hardly spare a pound of flesh	
	Tomorrow to my bloody creditor.	

SCENE III.
9. **naughty.** A strong word, not, as now, only reserved for children.—**fond:** foolish. 10. **To come abroad:** as to come abroad. Antonio has persuaded the jailer to let him walk out with his company. 19. **kept with:** resided with, associated with. 21. **His reason well I know.** Antonio interfered with Shylock's lending business by advancing money to deadbeats and thus rescuing Shylock's debtors from ruin (see 3.3.21ff. below). The money-lender in Shakespeare's day demanded security much greater than the value of the loan, expecting the property should become his if the loan went unpaid. We have previously had Shylock's own account of Antonio's maneuvering, which was probably distorted by hatred (see 3.1.40 ff.). 27. **commodity.** This word often means "advantage," sometimes "merchandise," and again "mercantilism." Here it seems to mean "'advantageous trade relations." The sense of the whole passage is "the Duke cannot forbid the law to take its course, without setting up a dangerous precedent for infringing on the rights of many other merchants engaged in international trade with Venice." The difficulty of the passage consists in making *commodity* the subject of *will impeach*. Legal rights to trade under the protection of the government will make the state vulnerable to charges of injustice if the law does not invariably take its course. 32. **bated me:** brought me out, reduced me in flesh. Antonio makes a feeble joke at his own expense.

Well, jailer, on. Pray God Bassanio come   35
To see me pay his debt, and then I care not!   *Exeunt.*

Scene IV. [*Belmont. Portia's house.*]

Enter Portia, Nerissa, Lorenzo, Jessica, *and* [Balthasar,] *a Man of Portia's.*

LOR.   Madam, although I speak it in your presence,
You have a noble and a true conceit
Of godlike amity, which appears most strongly
In bearing thus the absence of your lord.
But if you knew to whom you show this honor,   5
How true a gentleman you send relief,
How dear a lover of my lord your husband,
I know you would be prouder of the work
Than customary bounty can enforce you.

POR.   I never did repent for doing good,   10
Nor shall not now; for in companions
That do converse and waste the time together,
Whose souls do bear an egal yoke of love,
There must be needs a like proportion
Of lineaments, of manners, and of spirit;   *resemblance*   15
Which makes me think that this Antonio,
Being the bosom lover of my lord,
Must needs be like my lord. If it be so,
How little is the cost I have bestow'd
In purchasing the semblance of my soul   20
From out the state of hellish cruelty!
This comes too near the praising of myself.
Therefore no more of it. Hear other things.
Lorenzo, I commit into your hands
The husbandry and manage of my house   25
Until my lord's return. For mine own part,
I have toward heaven breath'd a secret vow
To live in prayer and contemplation,

Scene IV.
2. **conceit:** conception, idea. 9. **Than customary bounty,** etc.: The nobility of this particular act would make you prouder than any other act which you have undertaken by virtue of your usual goodness. 12. **converse:** associate.—**waste:** spend. 13. **egal...love:** Lovers who cherish equal amounts of love for each other, also may clone each other's physical and personality traits. [K.R.]14. **proportion:** symmetry, likeness. 15. **manners:** character. 17. **lover:** friend. 20. **the semblance of my soul:** i.e., Antonio. One who is the image of Bassanio, whom I love as I love my soul. 25. **husbandry and manage:** care and management.

                    Only attended by Nerissa here,
                    Until her husband and my lord's return.   30
                    There is a monastery two miles off,
                    And there we will abide. I do desire you
                    Not to deny this imposition,
                    The which my love and some necessity
                    Now lays upon you.

LOR.   Madam, with all my heart.   35
                    I shall obey you in all fair commands.

POR.   My people do already know my mind
                    And will acknowledge you and Jessica
                    In place of Lord Bassanio and myself.
                    So fare you well till we shall meet again.   40

LOR.   Fair thoughts and happy hours attend on you!

JES.   I wish your ladyship all heart's content.

POR.   I thank you for your wish, and am well pleas'd
                    To wish it back on you. Fare you well, Jessica.
                                                Exeunt [Jessica and Lorenzo].
                    Now, Balthasar,   45
                    As I have ever found thee honest-true,
                    So let me find thee still. Take this same letter,
                    And use thou all th' endeavour of a man
                    In speed to Padua. See thou render this
                    Into my cousin's hand, Doctor Bellario;   50
                    And look, what notes and garments he doth give thee,
                    Bring them, I pray thee, with imagin'd speed
                    Unto the Tranect, to the common ferry
                    Which trades to Venice. Waste no time in words
                    But get thee gone. I shall be there before thee.   55

BALTH.   Madam, I go with all convenient speed.[†]   *Exit.*

POR.   Come on, Nerissa. I have work in hand
                    That you yet know not of. We'll see our husbands
                    Before they think of us.

---

33. **Not to deny this imposition:** not to refuse this service that I impose upon you. 46. **honest-true:** honorable and trustworthy. Shakespeare is fond of such compound adjectives. 49. **render:** deliver. 51. **notes:** memoranda. 52. **imagin'd speed:** the speed of imagination. 53. **Tranect.** The word is explained in what follows, as the common ferry between Venice and the mainland. 56. **all convenient speed:** all speed that the means I can command will compass.

---

†   John Nolan, who plays Balthazar in the Nunn production, delivers this line with such airy condescension as to make his mistress look like a nagging scold. [K.R.]

NER.	Shall they see us?	
POR.	They shall, Nerissa, but in such a habit‡	60

That they shall think we are accomplished
With that we lack. I'll hold thee any wager,
When we are both accoutered like young men,
I'll prove the prettier fellow of the two,
And wear my dagger with the braver grace, *female → male* 65
And speak between the change of man and boy *to visit their*
With a reed voice, and turn two mincing steps *husbands in venice*
Into a manly stride; and speak of frays
Like a fine bragging youth; and tell quaint lies,
How honorable ladies sought my love, 70
Which I denying, they fell sick and died—
I could not do withal! Then I'll repent,
And wish, for all that, that I had not kill'd them.
And twenty of these puny lies I'll tell,
That men shall swear I have discontinued school 75
Above a twelvemonth. I have within my mind
A thousand raw tricks of these bragging Jacks,
Which I will practise.

NER.   Why, shall we turn to men?

POR. Fie, what a question's that,
If thou wert near a lewd interpreter! 80
But come, I'll tell thee all my whole device
When I am in my coach, which stays for us
At the park gate; and therefore haste away,
For we must measure twenty miles to-day.   *Exeunt.*

---

59. **Shall they see us?** *Us* is of course emphatic. Nerissa suspects that Portia intends to conceal herself or to assume a disguise. 61. **accomplished:** furnished. 62. **With that we lack:** male organs. 65. **braver grace:** finer grace. 67. **With a reed voice:** i.e., with a squeaky voice, like the note of a reed pipe. 69. **quaint:** elaborate. 72. **I could not do withal!** I could not help it—i.e., "I could not help their dying"—a regular idiom. 73. **for all that:** despite the fact that I could not help myself. 77. **Jacks:** fellows. (Portia here adopts the role of the *miles gloriosus*, braggart warrior, with many fierce but fictional tales of love and conquest.(K.R.).

‡ The disguising of Portia and Nerissa as young men introduces the stage convention of "cross-dressing," in which one sex pretends to be the other, though since all roles in the Elizabethan stage were played by boys or men anyway it did not then create the kind of erotic flavor that it does now. [K.R.]

SCENE V. [*Belmont. A garden.*]

Enter [Launcelot *the*] *Clown and* Jessica.

LAUN. Yes, truly; for look you, the sins of the father are to be laid upon the children. Therefore, I promise you, I fear you. I was always plain with you, and so now I speak my agitation of the matter. Therefore be o' good cheer, for truly I think you are damn'd. There is but one hope in it that can do you any good, and that is but a kind of bastard hope neither.   6

JES. And what hope is that, I pray thee?

LAUN. Marry, you may partly hope that your father got you not—that you are not the Jew's daughter.

JES. That were a kind of bastard hope indeed! So the sins of my mother should be visited upon me.   11

LAUN. Truly then I fear you are damn'd both by father and mother. Thus when I shun Scylla, your father, I fall into Charybdis, your mother. Well, you are gone both ways.

JES. I shall be sav'd by my husband. He hath made me a Christian.   15

LAUN. Truly, the more to blame he! We were Christians enow before, e'en as many as could well live one by another. This making of Christians will raise the price of hogs. If we grow all to be pork-eaters, we shall not shortly have a rasher on the coals for money.

Enter Lorenzo.

JES. I'll tell my husband, Launcelot, what you say. Here he comes.   20

LOR. I shall grow jealous of you shortly, Launcelot, if you thus get my wife into corners.

JES. Nay, you need not fear us, Lorenzo. Launcelot and I are out. He tells me flatly there's no mercy for me in heaven because I am a Jew's daughter; and he says you are no good member of the commonwealth, for in converting Jews to Christians you raise the price of pork.   26

SCENE V.
1. **the sins of the father,** etc. An obvious allusion to the Commandments. 2. **I fear you:** I fear for you. 3. **agitation.** Launcelot's mistake for *cogitation,* "thought," "opinion." 13. **Scylla...Charybdis:** two dangerous alternatives; in mythology, a monster and a whirlpool that threatened Odysseus and other mariners. [K.R.] 16. **We were Christians enow before:** i.e., "there were enough of us Christians before," "there were Christians enough in the world." 17. **one by another:** i.e., one off another. He means that Christians live on one another or by making profit out of one another. The joke that too many Christians, pork eaters, will raise the price of hogs is patently absurd, even tasteless [K.R.].

LOR.	I shall answer that better to the commonwealth than you can the getting up of the Negro's belly. The Moor is with child by you, Launcelot. 29
LAUN.	It is much that the Moor should be more than reason; but if she be less than an honest woman, she is indeed more than I took her for.
LOR.	How every fool can play upon the word! I think the best grace of wit will shortly turn into silence, and discourse grow commendable in none only but parrots. Go in, sirrah; bid them prepare for dinner.
LAUN.	That is done, sir. They have all stomachs. 35
LOR.	Goodly Lord, what a wit-snapper are you! Then bid them prepare dinner.
LAUN.	That is done too, sir. Only "cover" is the word.
LOR.	Will you cover then, sir?
LAUN.	Not so, sir, neither! I know my duty. 40
LOR.	Yet more quarrelling with occasion? Wilt thou show the whole wealth of thy wit in an instant? I pray thee understand a plain man in his plain meaning. Go to thy fellows, bid them cover the table, serve in the meat, and we will come in to dinner. 44
LAUN.	For the table, sir, it shall be serv'd in; for the meat, sir, it shall be cover'd; for your coming in to dinner, sir, why, let it be as humours and conceits shall govern. *Exit.*
LOR.	O dear discretion, how his words are suited! The fool hath planted in his memory An army of good words; and I do know 50 A many fools, that stand in better place, Garnish'd like him, that for a tricksy word Defy the matter. How cheer'st thou, Jessica? And now, good sweet, say thy opinion— How dost thou like the Lord Bassanio's wife? 55

---

33. **are out:** have quarrelled. 32. **the best grace of wit:** the most becoming form of wit. 38. **cover.** Launcelot means that the proper term to use is "to cover," i.e., to lay the table, instead of "to prepare dinner," as Lorenzo has said. 40. **Not so, sir, neither:** i.e., "no, I will not cover either,"—put on my cap. 41. **quarrelling with occasion:** abusing the opportunity to pun. 46-47. **as humours and conceits shall govern:** i.e., as your fancy and ideas shall prompt you. 48. **O dear discretion.** Lorenzo apostrophizes reason or common sense on account of the ludicrous folly of Launcelot's talk.—**suited:** dressed, dressed up. 51. **that stand in better place:** that occupy a higher rank in society. 52-53. **for a tricksy word Defy the matter:** i.e., have no regard for the sense of what they are talking about, provided they can work in a whimsical pun. This is Shakespeare's little fling at the punning fad of his time. The entire scene is a repository of flagrant punning and word play, in which Launcelot, the "wit-snapper" servant, in being the "inferior" person amuses everyone with his saucy insubordination. Punning is associated with oral cultures, the spoken spontaneous pun always being more effective than the written pun [K.R.]. 53. **How cheer'st thou?** i.e., "how dost thou feel?"

JES.   Past all expressing. It is very meet
                        The Lord Bassanio live an upright life;
                        For, having such a blessing in his lady,
                        He finds the joys of heaven here on earth;
                        And if on earth he do not merit it,   60
                        In reason he should never come to heaven.
                        Why, if two gods should play some heavenly match,
                        And on the wager lay two earthly women,
                        And Portia one, there must be something else
                        Pawn'd with the other; for the poor rude world   65
                        Hath not her fellow.

LOR.   Even such a husband
                        Hast thou of me as she is for a wife.

JES.   Nay, but ask my opinion too of that!

LOR.   I will anon. First let us go to dinner.

JES.   Nay, let me praise you while I have a stomach.   70

LOR.   No, pray thee, let it serve for table-talk;
                        Then, howsome'er thou speak'st, 'mong other things
                        I shall disgest it.

JES.   Well, I'll set you forth.   *Exeunt.*

---

63. **lay:** bet, stake. 64. **something else:** i.e., as boot, to make the wager equal. 67. **of me:** in me. 70. **stomach:** appetite—an obvious pun. "Let me praise you while I feel like it." 72. **howsome'er thou speak'st:** however ill you may speak of me. 73. **I'll set you forth:** I'll describe you finely. A playful threat which she intends to satirize on.

Act IV

Scene I. [*Venice. A court of justice.*]†

Enter the Duke, *the* Magnificoes, Antonio, Bassanio, Gratiano, [Solanio, *and others*].

Duke.	What, is Antonio here?
Ant.	Ready, so please your Grace.
Duke.	I am sorry for thee. Thou art come to answer

Duke.   I am sorry for thee. Thou art come to answer
A stony adversary, an inhuman wretch,
Uncapable of pity, void and empty   5
From any dram of mercy.

Ant.   I have heard
Your Grace hath ta'en great pains to qualify
His rigorous course; but since he stands obdurate,
And that no lawful means can carry me
Out of his envy's reach, I do oppose   10
My patience to his fury, and am arm'd
To suffer with a quietness of spirit
The very tyranny and rage of his.

Duke.   Go one, and call the Jew into the court.

Solan.   He is ready at the door; he comes, my lord.   15

Enter Shylock.

Duke.   Make room, and let him stand before our face.
Shylock, the world thinks, and I think so too,

Act IV. Scene I.
6. **dram:** insignificant amount 7. **qualify:** modify, soften. 9. **that:** i.e., since. It was common to use *that* rather than repeat *since* or *if.* 10. **his envy's reach:** out of the reach of his malignity or malice. 13. **The very tyranny and rage of his:** i.e., the full brunt of his savagery and wrath. 16. **our face.** The Duke uses the royal *we,* since this is a formal speech.

---

† The lengthy trial scene, whch is pivotal to the entire play and seals Shylock's fate, has by its dramatic power often seduced playgoers into thinking that it, rather than the lyric fifth act in Belmont, terminates the play. Little wonder then that directors have tended to spend enormous efforts in presenting it. The BBC version features a brightly lit court room with well dressed courtiers and ladies and ceremonious blasts of horns and trumpets accompanying the pomp and circumstance of the Duke's entrance. As Shylock, Warren Mitchell again dominates the action from the moment when he enters carrying a scale and a knife. In the Radford version, Al Pacino as Shylock occupies a crowded and cavernous room whose background has been made blurry by filters. The bare and sparse court room setting in the Nunn video leaves Henry Goodman's Shylock powerful but restrained and free from extraneous scenic embellishments. [K.R.]

That thou but leadest this fashion of thy malice
To the last hour of act; and then 'tis thought
Thou'lt show thy mercy and remorse more strange   20
Than is thy strange apparent cruelty;
And where thou now exacts the penalty,
Which is a pound of this poor merchant's flesh,
Thou wilt not only loose the forfeiture,
But, touch'd with humane gentleness and love,   25
Forgive a moiety of the principal,
Glancing an eye of pity on his losses,
That have of late so huddled on his back—
Enow to press a royal merchant down
And pluck commiseration of his state   30
From brassy bosoms and rough hearts of flint,
From stubborn Turks and Tartars, never train'd
To offices of tender courtesy.
We all expect a gentle answer, Jew.

SHY.   I have possess'd your Grace of what I purpose,   35
And by our holy Sabbath have I sworn
To have the due and forfeit of my bond.
If you deny it, let the danger light
Upon your charter and your city's freedom!
You'll ask me why I rather choose to have   40
A weight of carrion flesh than to receive
Three thousand ducats. I'll not answer that!
But say it is my humour, is it answer'd?
What if my house be troubled with a rat,
And I be pleas'd to give ten thousand ducats   45
To have it ban'd? What, are you answer'd yet?
Some men there are love not a gaping pig,
Some that are mad if they behold a cat,
And others, when the bagpipe sings i' th' nose,
Cannot contain their urine; for affection,   50

---

18. **this fashion of thy malice:** You have only pretended to be this malicious. 20. **remorse:** compassion. 22. **where:** whereas. 24. **loose:** release. 26. **moiety:** portion—not necessarily, as in modern English, "a half." 29. **a royal merchant down:** a merchant (or possibly his ship) with the resources of a kingdom at his back. *Royal* is the emphatic word. 33. **offices:** good offices. 35. **possess'd:** informed. 38, 39. **let the danger light,** etc. The point is that Venice can no longer be called a free city if it denies foreigners the rights that it guarantees them. Cf. Antonio's speech in 3.3. 26-31. 43. **humour:** whim, caprice. 47. **a gaping pig:** i.e., a roasted pig served at table, with an apple crammed into his open mouth, sometimes a feature at an English hunt breakfast. 48. **behold a cat.** Cf ., Increase Mather, *Illustrious Providences*, Boston, 1682, p. 101: "There are some who if a Cat accidently come into the Room, though they neither see it, nor are told of it, will presently be in a Sweat, and ready to die away." 50. **affection:** feeling, one's likes and dislikes.

Mistress of passion, sways it to the mood
Of what it likes or loathes. Now for your answer:
As there is no firm reason to be rend'red
Why he cannot abide a gaping pig,
Why he a harmless necessary cat,   55
Why he a woolen bagpipe—but of force
Must yield to such inevitable shame
As to offend himself, being offended;
So can I give no reason, nor I will not,
More than a lodg'd hate and a certain loathing   60
I bear Antonio, that I follow thus
A losing suit against him. Are you answer'd?

BASS.   This is no answer, thou unfeeling man,
To excuse the current of thy cruelty!

SHY.   I am not bound to please thee with my answers.   65

BASS.   Do all men kill the things they do not love?

SHY.   Hates any man the thing he would not kill?

BASS.   Every offence is not a hate at first.

SHY.   What, wouldst thou have a serpent sting thee twice?

ANT.   I pray you think you question with the Jew.   70
You may as well go stand upon the beach
And bid the main flood bate his usual height;
You may as well use question with the wolf,
Why he hath made the ewe bleat for the lamb;
You may as well forbid the mountain pines   75
To wag their high tops and to make no noise
When they are fretten with the gusts of heaven;
You may as well do anything most hard
As seek to soften that—than which what's harder?—
His Jewish heart. Therefore I do beseech you   80
Make no moe offers, use no farther means,
But with all brief and plain conveniency
Let me have judgment, and the Jew his will.

51, 52. **passion:** strong emotion.—**sways it to the mood/ Of what it likes or loathes.** The first *it* refers to *passion,* the second, to *affection.* A person's feelings will subtly influence the strongest emotions and irrationally support whimsical likes and dislikes. 53. **rend'red:** returned, given. 60. **certain:** fixed. 65 ff. Note this rapid dialogue of one-liners, each of which is sparked by its predecessor 70. **question:** talk. Perhaps "argue." 72. **the main flood:** the great sea. 77. **fretten:** fretted, worried, rubbed together. The verb *to fret* was a strong, or irregular, verb, meaning "to devour." Its meaning can be "to worry," or here "to torment by dashing or rubbing together." 82. **with all brief and plain conveniency:** with all acceptable brevity and directness.

BASS.	For thy three thousand ducats here is six.
SHY.	If every ducat in six thousand ducats 85 Were in six parts, and every part a ducat, I would not draw them, I would have my bond.
DUKE.	How shalt thou hope for mercy, rend'ring none?
SHY.	What judgment shall I dread, doing no wrong? You have among you many a purchas'd slave, 90 Which, like your asses and your dogs and mules, You use in abject and in slavish parts, Because you bought them. Shall I say to you, "Let them be free, marry them to your heirs! Why sweat they under burdens? Let their beds 95 Be made as soft as yours, and let their palates Be season'd with such viands"? You will answer, "The slaves are ours." So do I answer you. The pound of flesh which I demand of him Is dearly bought, 'tis mine, and I will have it. 100 If you deny me, fie upon your law! There is no force in the decrees of Venice. I stand for judgment. Answer. Shall I have it?
DUKE.	Upon my power I may dismiss this court Unless Bellario, a learned doctor, 105 Whom I have sent for to determine this, Come here today.
SOLAN.	My lord, here stays without A messenger with letters from the doctor, New come from Padua.
DUKE.	Bring us the letters. Call the messenger. 110
BASS.	Good cheer, Antonio! What, man, courage yet! The Jew shall have my flesh, blood, bones, and all, Ere thou shalt lose for me one drop of blood.
ANT.	I am a tainted wether of the flock, Meetest for death. The weakest kind of fruit 115 Drops earliest to the ground, and so let me. You cannot better be employ'd, Bassanio, Than to live still, and write mine epitaph.

---

87. **draw them:** take them. Cf. withdraw money from a bank. 92. **parts:** acts, services. With a suggestion of abusive behavior (K.R.). 114. **I am a tainted wether,** etc. A sick sheep, most likely to be killed first [K.R.]. Antonio's habitual melancholy surfaces from the beginning to the end of the play, whether he is in prosperity or adversity.

Enter Nerissa, *[dressed like a Lawyer's Clerk].*

Duke.	Came you from Padua from Bellario?
Ner.	From both, my lord. Bellario greets your Grace. [*Presents a letter.*] 120
Bass.	Why dost thou whet thy knife so earnestly?
Shy.	To cut the forfeiture from that bankrout there.
Gra.	Not on thy sole, but on thy soul, harsh Jew,
	Thou mak'st thy knife keen; but no metal can—
	No, not the hangman's axe—bear half the keenness 125
	Of thy sharp envy. Can no prayers pierce thee?
Shy.	No, none that thou hast wit enough to make.
Gra.	O, be thou damn'd, inexorable dog,
	And for thy life let justice be accus'd!
	Thou almost mak'st me waver in my faith, 130
	To hold opinion with Pythagoras,
	That souls of animals infuse themselves
	Into the trunks of men. Thy currish spirit
	Govern'd a wolf, who, hang'd for human slaughter,
	Even from the gallows did his fell soul fleet, 135
	And, whilst thou layest in thy unhallowed dam,
	Infus'd itself in thee; for thy desires
	Are wolvish, bloody, starv'd, and ravenous.
Shy.	Till thou canst rail the seal from off my bond,
	Thou but offend'st thy lungs to speak so loud. 140
	Repair thy wit, good youth, or it will fall
	To cureless ruin. I stand here for law.
Duke.	This letter from Bellario doth commend
	A young and learned doctor to our court.
	Where is he?
Ner.	He attendeth here hard by 145
	To know your answer whether you'll admit him.
Duke.	With all my heart. Some three or four of you
	Go give him courteous conduct to this place.

---

123. **Not on thy sole, but on thy soul.** This cliché of a pun was probably too threadbare to generate a robust laugh. 125. **bear:** have. 126. **envy:** malice, malignity. 128. **inexorable.** The word choice in the Quartos and the first two Folios is *inexecrable*. The Third and Fourth Folios have *inexorable*. Probably *inexecrable* is right and means "so execrable that it is impossible to curse thee enough." [k.r.] 129. **for thy life let justice be accus'd:** i.e., Your death can easily be explained as a simple act of justice. 131. **To hold opinion:** so as to agree with.—**Pythagoras.** Pythagoras may have introduced among the Greeks the doctrine of the transmigration of souls. 134. **who, hang'd.** , "and when he was hanged." 135. **fell:** cruel. 137. **in:** into. 142. **ruin.** Dissyllabic.

Meantime the court shall hear Bellario's letter.

[*Clerk reads.*] "Your Grace shall understand that at the receipt of your
    letter I am very sick; but in the instant that your messenger came,
    in loving visitation was with me a young doctor of Rome—his
    name is Balthasar. I acquainted him with the cause in controversy
    between the Jew and Antonio the merchant. We turn'd o'er
    many books together. He is furnished with my opinion, which,
    bettered with his own learning (the greatness whereof I cannot
    enough commend), comes with him at my importunity to fill
    up your Grace's request in my stead. I beseech you let his lack of
    years be no impediment to let him lack a reverend estimation;
    for I never knew so young a body with so old a head. I leave him
    to your gracious acceptance, whose trial shall better publish his
    commendation."   162

Enter Portia *for Balthasar,* [*dressed like a Doctor of Laws*].

DUKE.   You hear the learn'd Bellario what he writes;
           And here, I take it, is the doctor come.
           Give me your hand. Come you from old Bellario?   165

POR.   I did, my lord.

DUKE.   You are welcome; take your place.
           Are you acquainted with the difference
           That holds this present question in the court?

POR.   I am informed throughly of the cause.
           Which is the merchant here? and which the Jew?   170

DUKE.   Antonio and old Shylock, both stand forth.

POR.   Is your name Shylock?

SHY.   Shylock is my name.

POR.   Of a strange nature is the suit you follow;
           Yet in such rule that the Venetian law
           Cannot impugn you as you do proceed.—   175
           You stand within his danger, do you not?

---

150. **shall understand.** "Will, I am sure, understand." 152. **in loving visitation:** on a friendly visit.
159. **to let him lack:** Do not hold his youth against him. 161-62. **whose trial shall better publish
his commendation:** i.e., His own conduct will better reveal his skills than any mere description.
163. **You hear the learn'd Bellario what he writes.** Note the **prolepsis** in construction. (i.e., the
representation of a future event as if it had already happened). 168. **holds this present question.**
Are you familiar with the issues in this case? 175. **as you do proceed:** i.e., in the process, the method
of proceeding that you adopt. 176. **You stand within his danger** i.e., you are in his power (*Danger*
originally meant "domination," "lordship") though the laws of Venice guarantee your right to bring
suit without restriction.

ANT.	Ay, so he says.
POR.	Do you confess the bond?
ANT.	I do.
POR.	Then must the Jew be merciful.
SHY.	On what compulsion must I? Tell me that.

POR.   The quality of mercy is not strain'd;†   180
It droppeth as the gentle rain from heaven
Upon the place beneath. It is twice blest—
It blesseth him that gives, and him that takes.
'Tis mightiest in the mightiest. It becomes   *power over all*
The throned monarch better than his crown.   185
His sceptre shows the force of temporal power,
The attribute to awe and majesty,
Wherein doth sit the dread and fear of kings;
But mercy is above this sceptred sway;
It is enthroned in the hearts of kings,   190
It is an attribute to God himself;
And earthly power doth then show likest God's
When mercy seasons justice. Therefore, Jew,
Though justice be thy plea, consider this—
That, in the course of justice, none of us   195
Should see salvation. We do pray for mercy,
And that same prayer doth teach us all to render
The deeds of mercy. I have spoke thus much
To mitigate the justice of thy plea;
Which if thou follow, this strict court of Venice   200

---

179. **must.** This is the emphatic word. 180. **The quality of mercy is not strain'd.** *Quality* means "characteristic quality" or "nature" and *strained* means "constrained" (or restricted). The Jew has asked what compulsion makes it possible to say that he *must* be merciful. Portia replies that mercy's characteristic quality is not a matter of constraint, but spontaneity like the rain from heaven. 190. **in the hearts of kings.** *Hearts* is the emphatic word. 192. **show:** appear. 193. **seasons:** modifies, qualifies. 195. **in the course of justice,** etc. The regular doctrine that all men are justly condemned by God on account of Adam's trangression and that it is only through God's mercy that anybody can be saved. 198. **The deeds of mercy.** A prayer for mercy to us obliges us to act mercifully toward others.

---

†   Portia's speech on the "Quality of mercy" is a great aria in the midst of the courtroom scene. The fact that she ironically shows little mercy to Shylock has often been noted. Finding fresh ways to deliver this familiar speech presents a challenge to all actors.. In the Nunn version Derbhle Crotty rejects classroom elocution in favor of sitting down closely with Shylock, almost in the way that interrogators on TV detective shows question their quarry. An important part of the scene also involves Shylock's sadistic whetting of his knife and a general hostility in the court room toward the money lender, which in the BBC version is manifested by spectators trying to block his way to the front of the courtroom. Filmed from a low angle, the Duke (Douglas Wilmer) in the BBC version manages to convey an aura of complete authority. [K.R.]

	Must needs give sentence 'gainst the merchant there.	
SHY.	My deeds upon my head! I crave the law,	
	The penalty and forfeit of my bond.	
POR.	Is he not able to discharge the money?	
BASS.	Yes, here I tender it for him in the court;	205
	Yea, thrice the sum. If that will not suffice,	
	I will be bound to pay it ten times o'er	
	On forfeit of my hands, my head, my heart.	
	If this will not suffice, it must appear	
	That malice bears down truth. And I beseech you,	210
	Wrest once the law to your authority.	
	To do a great right, do a little wrong,	
	And curb this cruel devil of his will.	
POR.	It must not be. There is no power in Venice	
	Can alter a decree established.	215
	'Twill be recorded for a precedent;	
	And many an error by the same example	
	Will rush into the state. It cannot be.	
SHY.	A Daniel come to judgment! yea, a Daniel!	
	O wise young judge, how I do honor thee!	220
POR.	I pray you let me look upon the bond.	
SHY.	Here 'tis, most reverend Doctor, here it is.	
POR.	Shylock, there's thrice thy money off'red thee.	
SHY.	An oath, an oath, I have an oath in heaven!	
	Shall I lay perjury upon my soul?	225
	No, not for Venice.	
POR.	Why, this bond is forfeit;	
	And lawfully by this the Jew may claim	
	A pound of flesh, to be by him cut off	
	Nearest the merchant's heart. Be merciful.	
	Take thrice thy money; bid me tear the bond.	230
SHY.	When it is paid, according to the tenure.	
	It doth appear you are a worthy judge;	
	You know the law, your exposition	
	Hath been most sound. I charge you by the law,	

---

211. **Wrest once the law to your authority:** i.e., release Antonio, even if you have to bend the law to bring it into accord with your decree. 219. **A Daniel come to judgment:** The allusion is to the wisdom shown by the youthful Daniel in deciding the case between Susanna and the Elders, which may be found in that part of the book of Daniel included in the Apocrypha in King James's Version.

	Whereof you are a well-deserving pillar,	235
	Proceed to judgment. By my soul I swear	
	There is no power in the tongue of man	
	To alter me. I stay here on my bond.	
ANT.	Most heartily I do beseech the court	
	To give the judgment.	
POR.	Why then, thus it is:	240
	You must prepare your bosom for his knife.	
SHY.	O noble judge! O excellent young man!	
POR.	For the intent and purpose of the law	
	Hath full relation to the penalty,	
	Which here appeareth due upon the bond.	245
SHY.	'Tis very true. O wise and upright judge!	
	How much more elder art thou than thy looks!	
POR.	Therefore lay bare your bosom.	
SHY.	Ay, his breast—	
	So says the bond; doth it not, noble judge?	
	Nearest his heart. Those are the very words.	250
POR.	It is so. Are there balance here to weigh	
	The flesh?	
SHY.	I have them ready.	
POR.	Have by some surgeon, Shylock, on your charge,	
	To stop his wounds, lest he do bleed to death.	
SHY.	Is it so nominated in the bond?	255
POR.	It is not so express'd; but what of that?	
	'Twere good you do so much for charity.	
SHY.	I cannot find it; 'tis not in the bond.	
POR.	You, merchant, have you anything to say?	
ANT.	But little. I am arm'd and well prepar'd.	260
	Give me your hand, Bassanio. Fare you well!	
	Grieve not that I am fall'n to this for you;	
	For herein Fortune shows herself more kind	

---

238. **I stay here on my bond:** i.e., I abide by the provisions of my bond. 244. **Hath full relation to the penalty:** i.e., fully applies to any penalty, even that which is mentioned in the present bond. 247. **more elder.** In Elizabethan English, *elder* and *eldest* were interchangeable, with *older* and *oldest* In modern English they are confined to certain phrases like "eldest son," and the like. 251. **balance.** Plural, a condensed form of *balances* (scales). 253. **on your charge:** at your own expense. 260. **arm'd.** Much the same as "prepared."

Than is her custom. It is still her use
To let the wretched man outlive his wealth   265
To view with hollow eye and wrinkled brow
An age of poverty; from which ling'ring penance
Of such misery doth she cut me off.
Commend me to your honorable wife;
Tell her the process of Antonio's end;   270
Say how I lov'd you, speak me fair in death;
And when the tale is told, bid her be judge
Whether Bassanio had not once a love.
Repent but you that you shall lose your friend,
And he repents not that he pays your debt;   275
For if the Jew do cut but deep enough,
I'll pay it instantly with all my heart.

quitting picture

BASS.   Antonio, I am married to a wife
Which is as dear to me as life itself;
But life itself, my wife, and all the world   280
Are not with me esteem'd above thy life.
I would lose all, ay, sacrifice them all
Here to this devil, to deliver you.

POR.   Your wife would give you little thanks for that
If she were by to hear you make the offer.   285

GRA.   I have a wife who I protest I love.
I would she were in heaven, so she could
Entreat some power to change this currish Jew.

NER.   'Tis well you offer it behind her back.
The wish would make else an unquiet house.   290

SHY.   [*aside*] These be the Christian husbands! I have a daughter—
Would any of the stock of Barrabas
Had been her husband rather than a Christian!—
We trifle time. I pray thee pursue sentence.

POR.   A pound of that same merchant's flesh is thine.   295
The court awards it, and the law doth give it.

SHY.   Most rightful judge!

POR.   And you must cut this flesh from off his breast.
The law allows it, and the court awards it.

SHY.   Most learned judge! A sentence! Come, prepare!   300

---

268. **Of such misery** :Fortune saves him from the miseries of old age by taking his life. 269. **Commend me:** give my regards. 270. **the process:** the whole course of the matter. 274. **Repent but you:** i.e., if you feel regret for my loss, that makes me ready to die. 294. **We trifle time:** we waste time in trifling.

The refined and lady-like Portia cross-dressed as a male lawyer, Balthasar, suddenly in the trial scene turns into a formidable litigator as she confronts Shylock: "Prepare thee to cut off the flesh." (Nunn, 2001)

POR.	Tarry a little; there is something else.
	This bond doth give thee here no jot of blood;
	The words expressly are "a pound of flesh."
	Take then thy bond, take thou thy pound of flesh;
	But in the cutting it if thou dost shed 305
	One drop of Christian blood, thy lands and goods
	Are, by the laws of Venice, confiscate
	Unto the state of Venice.
GRA.	O upright judge! Mark, Jew. O learned judge!
SHY.	Is that the law?
POR.	Thyself shalt see the act; 310
	For, as thou urgest justice, be assur'd
	Thou shalt have justice more than thou desir'st.
GRA.	O learned judge! Mark, Jew. A learned judge!
SHY.	I take this offer then. Pay the bond thrice,
	And let the Christian go.
BASS.	Here is the money. 315
POR.	Soft!
	The Jew shall have all justice. Soft! no haste.
	He shall have nothing but the penalty.

---

311. **thou urgest justice:** thou makest justice thy plea. *To urge* often means "to mention." Here it may mean "to press," as in modern English. 316. **Soft!** slowly, don't be in a hurry.

GRA.   O Jew! an upright judge! a learned judge!

POR.   Therefore prepare thee to cut off the flesh.   320
       Shed thou no blood, nor cut thou less nor more
       But just a pound of flesh. If thou tak'st more
       Or less than a just pound—be it but so much
       As makes it light or heavy in the substance
       Or the division of the twentieth part   325
       Of one poor scruple; nay, if the scale do turn
       But in the estimation of a hair—
       Thou diest, and all thy goods are confiscate.

[handwritten margin note: literal nature of the law Jews are seen as being literal → portia taking this on]

GRA.   A second Daniel! a Daniel, Jew!
       Now, infidel, I have you on the hip.   330

POR.   Why doth the Jew pause? Take thy forfeiture.

SHY.   Give me my principal, and let me go.

BASS. I have it ready for thee; here it is.

POR.   He hath refus'd it in the open court.
       He shall have merely justice and his bond.   335

GRA.   A Daniel still say I, a second Daniel!
       I thank thee, Jew, for teaching me that word.

SHY.   Shall I not have barely my principal?

POR.   Thou shalt have nothing but the forfeiture,
       To be so taken at thy peril, Jew.   340

SHY.   Why, then the devil give him good of it!
       I'll stay no longer question.

POR.   Tarry, Jew.
       The law hath yet another hold on you.
       It is enacted in the laws of Venice,
       If it be prov'd against an alien   345
       That by direct or indirect attempts
       He seek the life of any citizen,
       The party 'gainst the which he doth contrive
       Shall seize one half his goods; the other half
       Comes to the privy coffer of the state;   350
       And the offender's life lies in the mercy
       Of the Duke only, 'gainst all other voice.
       In which predicament I say thou stand'st;

[handwritten margin note: oppressive nature of the law]

[handwritten margin note: christians are always defended]

---

323. **just:** exact. 330. **on the hip:** see note 36. 345. **alien.** Trisyllabic. 353. **In which predicament:** that is to say, in which category, or class of persons; so "in which situation." Now always used for a "bad situation."

	For it appears by manifest proceeding
	That indirectly, and directly too, 355
	Thou hast contriv'd against the very life
	Of the defendant, and thou hast incurr'd
	The danger formerly by me rehears'd.
	Down, therefore, and beg mercy of the Duke.
Gra.	Beg that thou mayst have leave to hang thyself! 360
	And yet, thy wealth being forfeit to the state,
	Thou hast not left the value of a cord;
	Therefore thou must be hang'd at the state's charge.
Duke.	That thou shalt see the difference of our spirit,
	I pardon thee thy life before thou ask it. 365
	For half thy wealth, it is Antonio's;
	The other half comes to the general state,
	Which humbleness may drive unto a fine.
Por.	Ay, for the state, not for Antonio.
Shy.	Nay, take my life and all! Pardon not that! 370
	You take my house when you do take the prop
	That doth sustain my house. You take my life
	When you do take the means whereby I live.
Por.	What mercy can you render him, Antonio?
Gra.	A halter gratis. Nothing else, for God's sake! 375
Ant.	So please my lord the Duke and all the court
	To quit the fine for one half of his goods,
	I am content; so he will let me have
	The other half in use, to render it
	Upon his death unto the gentleman 380
	That lately stole his daughter—
	Two things provided more: that, for this favour,
	He presently become a Christian;
	The other, that he do record a gift
	Here in the court of all he dies possess'd 385
	Unto his son Lorenzo and his daughter.

---

368. **humbleness may drive into a fine:** i.e., "if you bear yourself humbly, I may be induced to commute the forfeit of half of your goods to a mere fine." 369. **for the state, not for Antonio.** Portia carefully points out that the Duke has no authority to release Shylock from paying half his goods to Antonio. 371. **You take my life:** For many, denial of a right to practice a trade was in effect a sentence to death by slow starvation. 375. **A halter gratis:** a hangman's noose, at no charge. [K.R.] 376. **So please,** etc. If the Duke is willing to release Shylock from paying half his goods to the state, Antonio will be satisfied with the mere use of the other half during Shylock's lifetime instead of the legal reqirement of absolute possession, 383. **presently:** instantly. 385. **of all he dies possess'd:** i.e., possessed of. The preposition at the end of a clause is often omitted.

DUKE.	He shall do this, or else I do recant
	The pardon that I late pronounced here.
POR.	Art thou contented, Jew? What dost thou say?
SHY.	I am content.
POR.	Clerk, draw a deed of gift. 390
SHY.	I pray you give me leave to go from hence.
	I am not well. Send the deed after me,
	And I will sign it.
DUKE.	Get thee gone, but do it.
GRA.	In christ'ning shalt thou have two godfathers.
	Had I been judge, thou shouldst have had ten more, 395
	To bring thee to the gallows, not the font. *Exit [Shylock].*
DUKE.	Sir, I entreat you home with me to dinner.
POR.	I humbly do desire your Grace of pardon.
	I must away this night toward Padua,
	And it is meet I presently set forth. 400
DUKE.	I am sorry that your leisure serves you not.
	Antonio, gratify this gentleman,
	For in my mind you are much bound to him.
	Exeunt Duke and his Train.
BASS.	Most worthy gentleman, I and my friend
	Have by your wisdom been this day acquitted 405
	Of grievous penalties, in lieu whereof,
	Three thousand ducats, due unto the Jew,
	We freely cope your courteous pains withal.
ANT.	And stand indebted, over and above,
	In love and service to you evermore. 410
POR.	He is well paid that is well satisfied;
	And I, delivering you, am satisfied,
	And therein do account myself well paid.

---

390. **I am content:** Although theologically bullied with a coerced conversion to Christianity, Shylock is not economically treated with undue severity. He simply loses the income on half his property, which income he would not spend in any case. The other half remains his own, and the whole property is to go to his daughter when he dies. Although the terms are galling to Shylock's pride and self-respect, they are much milder than could have been expected, owing to Antonio's interposition. 395. **ten more.** Ten and two would make the ordinary number of a jury. In this passage, however, the allusion is rather to halberdiers or other officers conducting a criminal to the scaffold. 400. **presently:** instantly. 402. **gratify this gentleman:** i.e., give him an honorarium. The gentleman, of course, is Portia. 404. **I and my friend:** Bassanio identifies the cause of Antonio with his own, and very properly, since Antonio's debt was for his sake. 406. **in lieu whereof:** in return for which services. 408. **cope your courteous pains withal:** meet your endeavours with—i.e., wish to recompense them with.

	My mind was never yet more mercenary.	
	I pray you know me when we meet again.	415
	I wish you well, and so I take my leave.	
BASS.	Dear sir, of force I must attempt you further.	
	Take some remembrance of us as a tribute,	
	Not as a fee. Grant me two things, I pray you—	
	Not to deny me, and to pardon me.	420
POR.	You press me far, and therefore I will yield.	
	Give me your gloves, I'll wear them for your sake;	

[Bassanio takes off his gloves.]

	And for your love I'll take this ring from you.	
	Do not draw back your hand. I'll take no more;	
	And you in love shall not deny me this.	425
BASS.	This ring, good sir? Alas, it is a trifle!	
	I will not shame myself to give you this.	
POR.	I will have nothing else but only this;	
	And now methinks I have a mind to it.	
BASS.	There's more depends on this than on the value.	430
	The dearest ring in Venice will I give you,	
	And find it out by proclamation.	
	Only for this, I pray you pardon me.	
POR.	I see, sir, you are liberal in offers.	
	You taught me first to beg, and now methinks	435
	You teach me how a beggar should be answer'd.	
BASS.	Good sir, this ring was given me by my wife;	
	And when she put it on, she made me vow	
	That I should neither sell nor give nor lose it.	
POR.	That 'scuse serves many men to save their gifts.	440
	And if your wife be not a madwoman,	
	And know how well I have deserv'd this ring,	
	She would not hold out enemy for ever	
	For giving it to me. Well, peace be with you!	

Exeunt [Portia and Nerissa].

ANT.	My Lord Bassanio, let him have the ring.	445
	Let his deservings, and my love withal,	
	Be valued 'gainst your wive's commandëment.	

---

415. **know me when we meet again.** This apparently is merely a request for the honor of Antonio's and Bassanio's further acquaintance. Naturally, however, it contains an allusion to Portia's disguise. 425. **in love:** i.e., if you love me. 427. **to give:** by giving. 433. **for this:** as to this ring. 446. **withal:** at the same time.

BASS.	Go, Gratiano, run and overtake him.
	Give him the ring and bring him, if thou canst,
	Unto Antonio's house. Away! make haste. *Exit Gratiano.* 450
	Come, you and I will thither presently,
	And in the morning early will we both
	Fly toward Belmont. Come, Antonio. *Exeunt.*

SCENE II. [*Venice. A street.*]

Enter Portia *and* Nerissa, [*disguised as before*].

POR.	Enquire the Jew's house out, give him this deed,
	And let him sign it. We'll away tonight
	And be a day before our husbands home.
	This deed will be well welcome to Lorenzo.

Enter Gratiano.

GRA.	Fair sir, you are well o'erta'en. 5
	My Lord Bassanio, upon more advice,
	Hath sent you here this ring, and doth entreat
	Your company at dinner.
POR.	That cannot be.
	His ring I do accept most thankfully,
	And so I pray you tell him. Furthermore, 10
	I pray you show my youth old Shylock's house.
GRA.	That will I do.
NER.	Sir, I would speak with you.
	[*Aside to Portia*] I'll see if I can get my husband's ring,
	Which I did make him swear to keep for ever.
POR.	[*aside to Nerissa*] Thou mayst, I warrant. We shall have old swearing 15
	That they did give the rings away to men;
	But we'll outface them, and outswear them too.
	[*Aloud*] Away! make haste. Thou know'st where I will tarry.

---

453. **toward.** Distinctly dissyllabic.
SCENE II.
1. **this deed:** the deed of gift mentioned in 4.1.390. 5. **you are well o'erta'en:** I am glad to have overtaken you. Cf. "well met." 6. **upon more advice:** on further consideration. 15. **old swearing:** hard swearing. *Old* is common as an emphatic adjective.

NER.   Come, good sir, will you show me to this house?   *Exeunt.*

ACT V

SCENE I. [*Belmont. Grounds of Portia's house.*]

Enter Lorenzo *and* Jessica.

LOR.   The moon shines bright. In such a night as this,
            When the sweet wind did gently kiss the trees
            And they did make no noise—in such a night
            Troilus methinks mounted the Troyan walls
            And sigh'd his soul toward the Grecian tents,   5
            Where Cressid lay that night.

JES.   In such a night
            Did Thisbe fearfully o'ertrip the dew,
            And saw the lion's shadow ere himself,
            And ran dismay'd away.

LOR.   In such a night
            Stood Dido with a willow in her hand   10
            Upon the wild sea-banks, and waft her love
            To come again to Carthage.

JES.   In such a night
            Medea gathered the enchanted herbs
            That did renew old Æson.

LOR.   In such a night
            Did Jessica steal from the wealthy Jew,   15
            And with an unthrift love did run from Venice
            As far as Belmont.

JES.   In such a night

ACT V. SCENE I.
1 ff. Compared with Shylock's bitter diatribes, this romantic but competitive verbal contest between Jessica and Lorenzo (the idea is to see who can keep up the bright dialogue the longest), echoes the classical patterns of Virgil's Eclogues, and reflects the play's wide spectrum of emotional chords. 4. **Troilus:** the eponymous hero of Chaucer's narrative poem, and the Elizabethan ideal of a faithful lover—**Troyan:** old form for *Trojan,* used here to add to the scene's lyric quality. 5. **towárd.** Pronounced with the accent on the second syllable. 6. **Cressid:** Cressida—Troilus's unfaithful love. 7-14. **Thisbe, Dido, Medea**: Examples of deserted or star-crossed lovers from Greek mythology. [K.R.] 10. **a willow:** the sign of betrayed or forsaken love, or of bereavement in love. 11. **waft:** wafted—i.e., made signs by gently waving the soft willow branch. 16. **an unthrift love:** i.e., a love which made her indifferent to her father's worldly prosperity, or, it may refer to Lorenzo's precarious finances.

Did young Lorenzo swear he lov'd her well,
Stealing her soul with many vows of faith,
And ne'er a true one.

LOR.   In such a night   20
Did pretty Jessica (like a little shrow)
Slander her love, and he forgave it her.

JES.   I would out-night you, did no body come;
But, hark, I hear the footing of a man.

Enter [Stephano,] a Messenger.

LOR.   Who comes so fast in silence of the night?   25

MESS.   A friend.

LOR.   A friend? What friend? Your name, I pray you, friend?

MESS.   Stephano is my name, and I bring word
My mistress will before the break of day
Be here at Belmont. She doth stray about   30
By holy crosses, where she kneels and prays
For happy wedlock hours.

LOR.   Who comes with her?

MESS.   None but a holy hermit and her maid.
I pray you, is my master yet return'd?

LOR.   He is not, nor we have not heard from him.   35
But go we in, I pray thee, Jessica,
And ceremoniously let us prepare
Some welcome for the mistress of the house.

Enter [Launcelot, the] Clown.

LAUN.   Sola, sola! wo ha, ho! sola, sola!

LOR.   Who calls?   40

LAUN.   Sola! Did you see Master Lorenzo and Mistress Lorenzo? Sola, sola!

LOR.   Leave holloaing, man! Here.

LAUN.   Sola! Where? where?

---

21. **shrow**: shrew, bad-tempered woman. [K.R.] 22. The lyrics that deal with heart ache and vows in the duets sung by Lorenzo and Jessica run against the grain of romance. They do, however, offer a perfect backdrop for the deviousness of the ring plot. [K.R.] 23. **I would out-night you:** i.e., I would win out in this contest of comparisons, beginning "in such a night." 28. **Stepháno.** Here accented on the second syllable, Stepháno. Later Shakespeare learned the proper pronunciation for the word, for he has Stéphano in *The Tempest.* 30-31. **She doth stray about By holy crosses:** i.e., she is engaged in a pilgrimage for some special purpose from one holy shrine (marked by a cross) to another. 39. **Sola, sola!** Accent the last syllable. Launcelot enters, shouting at the top of his voice.

| Lor. | Here! | 44 |

Laun.   Tell him there's a post come from my master, with his horn full of good news. My master will be here ere morning.   *[Exit.]*

Lor.   Sweet soul, let's in, and there expect their coming.
And yet no matter. Why should we go in?
My friend Stephano, signify, I pray you,
Within the house, your mistress is at hand   50
And bring your music forth into the air.   *[Exit Stephano.]*
How sweet the moonlight sleeps upon this bank!
Here will we sit and let the sounds of music
Creep in our ears. Soft stillness and the night
Become the touches of sweet harmony.   55
Sit, Jessica. Look how the floor of heaven
Is thick inlaid with patens of bright gold.
There's not the smallest orb which thou behold'st
But in his motion like an angel sings,
Still quiring to the young-ey'd cherubins;   60
Such harmony is in immortal souls;
But whilst this muddy vesture of decay
Doth grossly close it in, we cannot hear it.   *[Enter Musicians.]*
Come, ho, and wake Diana with a hymn!
With sweetest touches pierce your mistress' ear   65
And draw her home with music. Play music.

Jes.   I am never merry when I hear sweet music.

Lor.   The reason is, your spirits are attentive.
For do but note a wild and wanton herd,
Or race of youthful and unhandled colts,   70

---

45. **his horn.** The post rider sounds his horn to alert the stable hands to his imminent arrival and subsequent instant departure. Launcelot jests by comparing this horn to a cornucopia or horn of plenty. 49. Note the accent on *Stephano.* 54. **in:** into. 55. **Become:** are suited to.—**touches.** This contains an obvious allusion to the production of music by touching the instrument. *Touch your instrument* was equivalent to "play upon it." At the same time, the noun *touch* is often used for "peculiarity," "quality," and that meaning may also be intended here. 57. **patens:** tiles. 59. **in his motion like an angel sings:** i.e., makes sacred music by means of its physical motions, which contributed to the "music of the singing spheres." The various spheres of the Ptolemaic astronomy as they moved about the earth in harmonious though complicated circuits were thought to produce divine music. The theory was, as Lorenzo here explains, that despite the many poetic references to the music of the spheres, mortal ears were too dull to hear it. 60. **Still:** ever. 61. **Such harmony is in immortal souls:** i.e., our immortal souls are capable of hearing and appreciating this harmony, for it coincides in them with the great order of the universe. 63. **grossly:** with the gross substance of mortal flesh, which obstructs the senses of the soul. 64. **Diana.** Mentioned here because she is identified with the moon. Note that the moonlight is said to sleep in line 52. 65. **touches.** Cf. note on line 55. 68. **your spirits are attentive:** i.e., they are brought to attention to the music and so it is possible that they should have free play as they must do when one is merry. Cf. our phrases, "a flow of spirits," "animal spirits," and the like. 69. **wanton:** unpredictable, unbroken, untrained. 70: **unhandled:** untamed—i.e., never brought under the hands of man.

Fetching mad bounds, bellowing and neighing loud,
Which is the hot condition of their blood:
If they but hear perchance a trumpet sound,
Or any air of music touch their ears,
You shall perceive them make a mutual stand,   75
Their savage eyes turn'd to a modest gaze
By the sweet power of music. Therefore the poet
Did feign that Orpheus drew trees, stones, and floods,
Since naught so stockish, hard, and full of rage
But music for the time doth change his nature.   80
The man that hath no music in himself,
Nor is not mov'd with concord of sweet sounds,
Is fit for treasons, stratagems, and spoils;
The motions of his spirit are dull as night,
And his affections dark as Erebus.   85
Let no such man be trusted. Mark the music.

Enter Portia *and* Nerissa.

POR.   That light we see is burning in my hall.
        How far that little candle throws his beams!
        So shines a good deed in a naughty world.

NER.   When the moon shone, we did not see the candle.   90

POR.   So doth the greater glory dim the less.
        A substitute shines brightly as a king
        Until a king be by; and then his state
        Empties itself, as doth an inland brook
        Into the main of waters. Music! hark!   95

NER.   It is your music, madam, of the house.

POR.   Nothing is good, I see, without respect.
        Methinks it sounds much sweeter than by day.

NER.   Silence bestows that virtue on it, madam.

POR.   The crow doth sing as sweetly as the lark   100

---

72. **condition:** character, nature. 75. **You shall perceive:** i.e., "it will be clearly demonstrated to you." 76. **modest:** gentle, moderate, calm. 79. **stockish:** like a block of wood, blockish, dull. 83. **stratagems.** *Stratagem* was often used in the sense of a "dreadful deed," implying some intricate and sinister scheme, such as tunneling under and then blowing up an enemy fortification. 84. **motions of his spirit.** *Motions* is a common word for the operations of the mind and heart. 85. **affections:** feelings, motives—not precisely in the modern sense of warm feelings. 87. **That light,** etc. The conversation of Portia and Nerissa remains in the same gentle key as that of the other characters, who have been enchanted by the moonlight. Launcelot of course remains the loud-mouthed exception. 89. **naughty:** wicked. 93. **state:** dignity, majesty. 95. **the main of waters:** the great ocean. 97. **Nothing is good, I see, without respect.** "Nothing is absolutely good in itself, provided the circumstances under which one experiences it are not entirely favorable."

When neither is attended; and I think
The nightingale, if she should sing by day
When every goose is cackling, would be thought
No better a musician than the wren.
How many things by season season'd are   105
To their right praise and true perfection!
Peace, ho! The moon sleeps with Endymion,
And would not be awak'd.   *Music ceases.*

Lor.   That is the voice,
Or I am much deceiv'd, of Portia.

Por.   He knows me as the blind man knows the cuckoo,   110
By the bad voice.

Lor.   Dear lady, welcome home.

Por.   We have been praying for our husbands' welfare,
Which speed, we hope, the better for our words.
Are they return'd?

Lor.   Madam, they are not yet;
But there is come a messenger before   115
To signify their coming.

Por.   Go in, Nerissa.
Give order to my servants that they take
No note at all of our being absent hence—
Nor you, Lorenzo—Jessica, nor you.   *A tucket sounds.*

Lor.   Your husband is at hand; I hear his trumpet.   120
We are no telltales, madam; fear you not.

Por.   This night methinks is but the daylight sick;
It looks a little paler. 'Tis a day
Such as the day is when the sun is hid.

        Enter Bassanio, Antonio, Gratiano, *and their Followers.*

Bass.   We should hold day with the Antipodes   125
If you would walk in absence of the sun.

---

105. **How many things by season season'd are:** "How many things are brought to their proper reputation and perfection by virtue of their happening at the proper time!" 107. **Peace, ho!** Here Portia raises her voice in order to be heard by the musicians.—**Endymion**: the mortal lover of the goddess Diana, represented by the moon. [K.R.] 112. **We have been praying.** Portia has been pretending to go on a pilgrimage. See lines 30-32 above. 112. **speed:** prosper. 117-18. **that they take No note at all:** i.e., that they do not notice in any way, so that Bassanio and Gratiano may observe it. 119. **tucket:** a succession of notes on the trumpet, announcing the approach of a person of importance. 125. **We should hold day with the Antipodes,** etc.: We should be able to have it daylight here when our Antipodes do (i.e., when it is night with us), if you would only go abroad to illumine the earth. Bassanio announces his arrival with this pretty compliment, not supposing that Portia knows that he has overheard what she has said in lines 122-123.

POR.	Let me give light, but let me not be light;
	For a light wife doth make a heavy husband,
	And never be Bassanio so for me.
	But God sort all! You are welcome home, my lord. 130
BASS.	I thank you, madam. Give welcome to my friend.
	This is the man, this is Antonio,
	To whom I am so infinitely bound.
POR.	You should in all sense be much bound to him,
	For, as I hear, he was much bound for you. — *literally too* 135
ANT.	No more than I am well acquitted of.
POR.	Sir, you are very welcome to our house.
	It must appear in other ways than words,
	Therefore I scant this breathing courtesy.
GRA.	[*to Nerissa*] By yonder moon I swear you do me wrong! 140
	In faith, I gave it to the judge's clerk.
	Would he were gelt that had it, for my part,
	Since you do take it, love, so much at heart.
POR.	A quarrel, ho, already! What's the matter?
GRA.	About a hoop of gold, a paltry ring 145
	That she did give to me, whose posy was
	For all the world like cutler's poetry
	Upon a knife, "Love me, and leave me not."
NER.	What talk you of the posy or the value?
	You swore to me, when I did give it you, 150
	That you would wear it till your hour of death,
	And that it should lie with you in your grave.
	Though not for me, yet for your vehement oaths,
	You should have been respective and have kept it.
	Gave it a judge's clerk! No, God's my judge, 155
	The clerk will ne'er wear hair on's face that had it.
GRA.	He will, an if he live to be a man.
NER.	Ay, if a woman live to be a man.

127. **be light:** i.e., unfaithful. 128. **heavy:** sad. 130. **God sort all!** i.e., may God adjust everything as it should be. 134. **in all sense:** i.e., in accordance with all the dictates of reason. 136. **acquitted of:** cleared of. 139. **this breathing courtesy:** this courtesy that consists merely of breath—i.e., in words. 142. **for my part:** so far as I am concerned. 146. **posy:** the inscription on a ring. The word is contracted from *poesy*, since such mottoes were often, though not always, in verse. 149. **What talk you?** Why talk you? 154. **respective:** regardful.

portia gets revenge—turns Ant into a preist??

GRA.   Now, by this hand, I gave it to a youth,
        A kind of boy, a little scrubbed boy,   160
        No higher than thyself, the judge's clerk,
        A prating boy that begg'd it as a fee.
        I could not for my heart deny it him.

POR.   You were to blame—I must be plain with you—
        To part so slightly with your wive's first gift,   165
        A thing stuck on with oaths upon your finger
        And so riveted with faith unto your flesh.
        I gave my love a ring, and made him swear
        Never to part with it; and here he stands.
        I dare be sworn for him he would not leave it   170
        Nor pluck it from his finger for the wealth
        That the world masters. Now, in faith, Gratiano,
        You give your wife too unkind a cause of grief.
        An 'twere to me, I should be mad at it.

BASS.   [aside] Why, I were best to cut my left hand off   175
        And swear I lost the ring defending it.

GRA.   My Lord Bassanio gave his ring away
        Unto the judge that begg'd it, and indeed
        Deserv'd it too; and then the boy, his clerk,
        That took some pains in writing, he begg'd mine;   180
        And neither man nor master would take aught
        But the two rings.

POR.   What ring gave you, my lord?
        Not that, I hope, which you receiv'd of me.

BASS.   If I could add a lie unto a fault,
        I would deny it; but you see my finger   185
        Hath not the ring upon it—it is gone.

POR.   Even so void is your false heart of truth.
        By heaven, I will ne'er come in your bed
        Until I see the ring!

NER.   Nor I in yours
        Till I again see mine!

---

160. **a little scrubbed boy:** i.e., a little scrubby boy, as we call a *dwarf oak* a "scrub oak." The audience should be much amused at this description, since Gratiano has no idea that the original little scrubbed boy is listening, for indeed Gratiano is describing his own Nerissa. 164. **You were to blame:** you were culpable, blameworthy. 168. **I gave my love a ring.** Of course the pronouns are more or less emphatic. 173. Note the meter. 174. **An:** if.—**mad:** frantic—not merely "angry," in our modern colloquial sense of the term. 175. **I were best:** it would be best for me. 180. **That took some pains in writing:** that had done some service as a scribe or clerk, and so deserved a reward. 189. Portia's ruthless esposure of Bassanio's "faithfulness" ensures her future control over this amiable but possibly footloose young man. [K.R.]

BASS.   Sweet Portia,   190
    If you did know to whom I gave the ring,
    If you did know for whom I gave the ring,
    And would conceive for what I gave the ring,
    And how unwillingly I left the ring
    When naught would be accepted but the ring,   195
    You would abate the strength of your displeasure.

POR.   If you had known the virtue of the ring,
    Or half her worthiness that gave the ring,
    Or your own honor to contain the ring,
    You would not then have parted with the ring.   200
    What man is there so much unreasonable,
    If you had pleas'd to have defended it
    With any terms of zeal, wanted the modesty
    To urge the thing held as a ceremony?
    Nerissa teaches me what to believe.   205
    I'll die for't but some woman had the ring!

BASS.   No, by my honor, madam, by my soul,
    No woman had it, but a civil doctor,
    Which did refuse three thousand ducats of me
    And begg'd the ring; the which I did deny him,   210
    And suffer'd him to go displeas'd away,
    Even he that had held up the very life
    Of my dear friend. What should I say, sweet lady?
    I was enforc'd to send it after him.
    I was beset with shame and courtesy.   215
    My honor would not let ingratitude
    So much besmear it. Pardon me, good lady;
    For, by these blessed candles of the night,
    Had you been there, I think you would have begg'd
    The ring of me to give the worthy doctor.   220

POR.   Let not that doctor e'er come near my house.
    Since he hath got the jewel that I lov'd,
    And that which you did swear to keep for me,
    I will become as liberal as you;
    I'll not deny him anything I have,   225
    No, not my body, nor my husband's bed.

---

193. **And would conceive:** i.e., and would only give yourself the trouble of really understanding. 199. **to contain:** withhold. 203. **terms of zeal:** earnest words. 203-04. **wanted the modesty /To urge:** i.e., was so immodest or inconsiderate as to press for the possession of, to insist on. 204. **held as a ceremony:** kept by you as a ceremonial ring—i.e., a sacred pledge. 208. **a civil doctor:** i.e., a doctor of law. 215. **I was beset with shame and courtesy:** i.e., feelings of shame and of regard for politeness both attacked me.

	Know him I shall, I am well sure of it.
	Lie not a night from home; watch me like Argus.
	If you do not, if I be left alone,
	Now, by mine honor, which is yet mine own,
	I'll have that doctor for my bedfellow.
NER.	And I his clerk. Therefore be well advis'd
	How you do leave me to mine own protection.
GRA.	Well, do you so. Let not me take him then;
	For if I do, I'll mar the young clerk's pen.
ANT.	I am th' unhappy subject of these quarrels.
POR.	Sir, grieve not you. You are welcome notwithstanding.
BASS.	Portia, forgive me this enforced wrong, *debt + love*
	And in the hearing of these many friends
	I swear to thee, even by thine own fair eyes,
	Wherein I see myself—
POR.	Mark you but that?
	In both my eyes he doubly sees himself;
	In each eye one. Swear by your double self,
	And there's an oath of credit.
BASS.	Nay, but hear me.
	Pardon this fault, and by my soul I swear
	I never more will break an oath with thee.
ANT.	I once did lend my body for his wealth,
	Which, but for him that had your husband's ring,
	Had quite miscarried. I dare be bound again,
	My soul upon the forfeit, that your lord
	Will never more break faith advisedly.
POR.	Then you shall be his surety. *priest* Give him this,
	And bid him keep it better than the other.
ANT.	Here, Lord Bassanio. Swear to keep this ring.
BASS.	By heaven, it is the same I gave the doctor!
POR.	I had it of him. Pardon me, Bassanio;
	For, by this ring, the doctor lay with me.

Line numbers: 230 (at "Now, by mine honor"), 235 (at "For if I do"), 240 (at "I swear to thee"), 245 (at "Pardon this fault"), 250 (at "My soul upon the forfeit"), 255 (at "By heaven, it is the same").

---

228. **Argus**: In mythology, a hundred-eyed monster; he was an effective guardian because some of his eyes remained awake while others slept. [K.R.] 232. **be well advis'd**: be very careful. 238. **this enforced wrong**: this wrongful act that I was obliged to do. 243. **your double self.** With a pun on *double* in the sense of deceitful. 244. **an oath of credit**: an oath that may well be believed. Said ironically. 246. **for his wealth**: i.e., to make him rich. 249. **Had quite miscarried**: would have been utterly destroyed or lost. 250. **My soul upon the forfeit.** Absolute construction, "my soul being risked as the forfeit." 251. **advisedly**: deliberately.

At this key moment in the play, Portia (Lynn Collins) relieves Bassanio (Joseph Fiennes) of his guilt over having given away the ring to Balthasar (who is Portia in disguise), and informs Antonio (Jeremy Irons) that his ships have been saved. At the same time she manages to retain her powerful control over all the other characters. (Radford, 2004)

NER.	And pardon me, my gentle Gratiano;
	For that same scrubbed boy, the doctor's clerk,
	In lieu of this, last night did lie with me. 260
GRA.	Why, this is like the mending of highways
	In summer, where the ways are fair enough.
	What, are we cuckolds ere we have deserv'd it?
POR.	Speak not so grossly. You are all amaz'd.
	Here is a letter, read it at your leisure; 265
	It comes from Padua from Bellario.
	There you shall find that Portia was the doctor,
	Nerissa there her clerk. Lorenzo here
	Shall witness I set forth as soon as you,
	And even but now return'd. I have not yet 270
	Enter'd my house. Antonio, you are welcome,
	And I have better news in store for you
	Than you expect. Unseal this letter soon.
	There you shall find three of your argosies
	Are richly come to harbour suddenly. 275
	You shall not know by what strange accident

261-62. **Why, this is like,** etc.: to mend the roads when they are good enough is of course to make the roads bad, since no road is in good condition when it is being mended. Gratiano means that matters were in a better condition as they were before than they are now, after the revelation that Portia and Nerissa have made. 264. **amaz'd:** in a state of utter confusion. *All* is adverbial here. 276. **by what strange accident.** Portia chooses to make a mystery of the matter, and thus it becomes unnecessary to explain to the audience, who are willing to take it as her whim, but might otherwise wish to know the facts.

	I chanced on this letter.	
Ant.	I am dumb.	
Bass.	Were you the doctor, and I knew you not?	
Gra.	Were you the clerk that is to make me cuckold?	
Ner.	Ay, but the clerk that never means to do it, Unless he live until he be a man.	280
Bass.	Sweet Doctor, you shall be my bedfellow. When I am absent, then lie with my wife.	
Ant.	Sweet lady, you have given me life and living; For here I read for certain that my ships Are safely come to road.	285
Por.	How now, Lorenzo? My clerk hath some good comforts too for you.	
Ner.	Ay, and I'll give them him without a fee. There do I give to you and Jessica, From the rich Jew, a special deed of gift, After his death, of all he dies possess'd of.	290
Lor.	Fair ladies, you drop manna in the way Of starved people.	
Por.	It is almost morning,† And yet I am sure you are not satisfied Of these events at full. Let us go in;	295

---

286. **come to road:** come to the place where they lie at anchor. A *road* is a roadstead or anchorage. 293. **Of starved people.** Lorenzo, though a gentleman, was poor. This accounts for his calling himself an "unthrift love" in line 16. 294-95. **satisfied Of these events at full:** i.e., so fully informed about all these occurrences as to feel no further curiosity.

---

† Another of the great problems confronting the directors of *Merchant* is the blocking of the characters on stage for the ending of the play. Axiomatically, comedy involves the bringing together and festive reunion of all the characters. In *Merchant* there is the awkward situation of Antonio, who by the end of the play has found no congenial companion, and there is also uncertainty about the fitness of Jessica, who has betrayed her father, for acceptance in polite society. In neither instance is there any suggestion of Antonio or Jessica being condemned as "scapegoats" like Malvolio in *Twelfth Night*. In the BBC version everyone greets Antonio warmly, and in a gesture of solidarity he is allowed to read the letter announcing that his endangered ships have safely returned to harbor. When the socially acceptable couples (Portia and Bassanio, Nerissa and Gratiano) file off stage, Jessica starts to follow with Lorenzo but momentarily pauses, as if to acknowledge that her sin in betraying her father puts her in social purgatory. Antonio is left by himself and soon gravitates toward the faux pastoral set in which he began the play. No director goes to greater lengths to integrate the characters than Michael Radford, who in his film actually shows Jessica on a beach wearing the allegedly discarded turquoise ring. She watches fishermen whose simple labor perhaps symbolizes the tranquility that everyone desires. [k.r.]

And charge us there upon inter'gatories,
And we will answer all things faithfully.

GRA.   Let it be so. The first inter'gatory
That my Nerissa shall be sworn on is,
Whether till the next night she had rather stay,   300
Or go to bed now, being two hours to day.
But were the day come, I should wish it dark
Till I were couching with the doctor's clerk.
Well, while I live I'll fear no other thing   304
So sore as keeping safe Nerissa's ring.   *Exeunt.*

---

298. **charge us there upon inter'gatories:** i.e., load us with whatever questions you like, impose whatever questions you wish upon us.

HOW TO READ *THE MERCHANT OF VENICE* AS PERFORMANCE

Who *reads* a play? We *hear* plays, *listen* to plays, *see* plays, *watch* plays, *go* to plays. Unless you are a Broadway producer or a film editor, you don't ordinarily read play scripts. As a student of Shakespeare, however, you will inevitably *study* a Shakespeare play in print. Particularly before attending a play that you are a bit fuzzy about, and whose language you may find confusing, an advance reading is a very good idea. Close reading of the text will soon lead to consideration of the key elements in dramaturgy, as long ago defined by Aristotle, of language, plot, character, spectacle, theme, and finally, if applicable, music.

The more that is known in advance about a play, the more satisfying the reading. Plot outlines make a good beginning for getting the major shape in mind, and also useful is a photocopy of the play's *dramatis personae* to avoid having to thumb back through the pages in search of the cast list. Reading while listening to a recording such as the one of *The Merchant of Venice* in the new Arkangel-Penguin series forces attention on the language. The Arkangel *Merchant* features Trevor Peacock as a wily Shylock and Hadyn Gwynne as Portia, with Dominique Le Gendre's original score providing compelling sonic help. In the absence of a recording, reading the play aloud, alone or in company, also enforces attention and highlights textual problems. A convenient glossary of difficult words may prove a Godsend as you navigate through the work of an author with a vocabulary of about 35, 000 words, many of which are now archaic, or which Shakespeare sprinkled with suffixes and prefixes, like "ennoble," "unus'd, " "forebemoaned,"etc..

One shibboleth should be confronted right away. For the inexperienced, reading Shakespeare is not exactly "fun," any more than climbing Mount Everest is fun. The "fun" comes in with the sense of pleasure and achievement at conquering a challenge. Another thing to remember is that Shakespeare wrote in early Modern English, not Middle English (the language of Chaucer), and not Old English (the language of the *Beowulf* epic). Finally, today's reader of Shakespeare benefits from an electronic revolution that has put a galaxy of televised and cinematic productions, on VHS and DVD, available at almost any video rental outlet. The most ambitious, though not the most successful, would be the complete BBC/Time/Life Shakespeare plays that cast dozens of outstanding British actors, but regrettably included almost no North Americans. Even newer technologies like iPod , Google, and YouTube have scanned miraculous amounts of data, a great deal of which was in the past often found only in the archives of inaccessible libraries. Google offers early texts like the 1600 Quarto of *Merchant,* which previously had been sequestered in library rare book rooms. YouTube makes an Italian 1910 silent *Merchant* available on a computer screen, or, among dozens of other entries, the Radford *Merchant* with Italian dialogue.

In drama, language provides the catalyst for bringing together the interaction between plot and character that establishes the play's major themes. Until a character is actually tested in a conflict of some sort there is, as in life, no character, but only a hollow vessel. Mastering the play's language may lead to an unexpected sense of *Schadenfreude,* the German word for taking pleasure in watching another human being stumble, as when in a major production Morocco proclaims "All that *glistens* is not gold" when it should be, as you knew from independent reading, "All that *glisters* is not gold" (2.7.65). Reading allows time to master the full meaning of a passage, which in the theatre may scoot by unheard, either through an actor's poor enunciation or the listener's own fatigue.

An example of this problem occurs with Shylock's speech on tolerance that ranks, along with the Ten Commandments, the Gettysburg Address, and the Sacco and Vanzetti letters, among liberalism's most sacred documents:

"I am a Jew. Hath not a Jew eyes? Hath not a Jew hands, organs, dimensions, senses, affections, passions…If you prick us, do we not bleed? If you tickle us, do we not laugh? If you poison us, do we not die? (*MV* 3.1.42ff.)

Ever since actors began playing on audience sympathy for Shylock, there has been a tendency to credit Shylock with the sensibility of a liberal democrat, though scrutiny of the entire speech shows an underlying current of malice as he declares that "the villainy you teach me I will execute, and it shall go hard but I will better the instruction" (3.1.52-3). The point is that a skilful actor like Al Pacino can wring multiple insinuations out of a speech. The spectator who knows the text will be better prepared to appreciate its literal meaning and its underlying implications, or subtext, not so much what the actor *says* as what he *thinks.* To put it another way, the meaning *between* the lines can be as important as the meaning *in* the lines. A very significant clue can also be teased out from the way that an actor responds to another actor's words, through facial expressions and body language. Both the onstage and the offstage audience may feel uneasy about the reckless way that Antonio puts "a pound" of his own flesh in jeopardy while seeming to buy into Shylock's attempt to pass off the bizarre agreement as a "merry jest." Antonio does not have a clue, saying "Yes, Shylock, I will seal unto this bond" (1.3.161), despite Bassanio's warning: "You shall not seal such a bond for me"(1.3.144). The entire sequence is a mini-play-within-a-play in its micro-enactment of a major theme of *The Merchant of Venice,* which is the conflict between prodigality and avarice. This one exchange challenges the reader to pay attention to Shylock's tone of voice, Antonio's heedlessness. and Bassanio's wariness. The way in which each character responds to this twist in the plot defines his character. The gap between Shylock's outward lightheartedness and his inner malice, in so far as it can be detected by the offstage audience, is an example of *dramatic irony*—a situation in which the audience knows more about the events on stage than do the actors themselves.

The frequent exhortations by teachers to imagine the staging of a play in one's own mind does not conceal the magnitude of the task, There is the need to conjure up images of the stage design, the players' costumes, the expressions on the actors' faces, the choreography, the timing of exits and entrances, and to do so while struggling to read the play accurately line by line for a class assignment. This strenuous activity will, however, enhance the quality of a theatrical experience. *The Merchant* actually begins in mystery with Antonio's depressed state of mind: "In sooth I know not why I am so sad./It wearies me, you say it wearies you"(1.1.1). The exact cause of his melancholy is never made explicit, though it could derive from his business worries (he has merchant ships on perilous seas), his loneliness (he is a bachelor), his erotic attachment to Bassanio (who is more interested in Portia than in Antonio), a chemical imbalance (according to some modern psychological theories), or none of the above. Subsequent allusions in Salerio's speeches reinforce these speculations. Sea images of "tossing" and "dangerous rocks" suggest risk and the great line, "Enrobe the roaring waters with my silks" (1.1.34) shadows forth the thin line between bourgeois opulence and the savage forces threatening it. The risks of the sea and the hazards of business in Venice echo each other. Gratiano's comment that "they lose it that do buy it with much care" (1.1.75) adds to the sense of a world dedicated to profit and loss. The line comes to mind from Matt. 16:26: What shall it profit a man to gain the whole world and lose his own soul? That in turn gets at Shylock, who values his business dealings more than anything else. And yet this is only "one side" of Shylock, for elsewhere the script makes plain a fierce attachment to his daughter, Jessica.

Still another method of determining character comes through the device of one character describing another, which is exactly what Portia does with her suitors in describing the Neapolitan prince, County Palatine, Monsieur Le Bon, The English baron Falconridge, the Scottish Lord and the young German (1.2.29ff.). (In the Trevor Nunn version there is a clever modernization as Nerissa shows moving images of Portia's suitors on a 16mm movie projector). The themes of the play become interlocked in this single incident. Portia's fierce dedication to the wording of her father's will ("I will die...unless / I be obtain'd by the manner of my father's will" (1.3.77-78) ironically mirrors Shylock's obsession with legalisms over the pound of flesh. ("I have sworn an oath that I will have my bond" (3.3.5).

It soon emerges that almost any sub-section of a Shakespearean play echoes, or mirrors, many other sections; that the play itself enfolds a variety of mini-plays, each one corresponding to a theme in the main play. The analogy might be to one of those Russian dolls that conceal within themselves layer after layer of replicas of themselves. One example is the way that Launcelot Gobbo's strange relationship with his father mirrors the parent-daughter relationships between Portia and Jessica and their fathers. None of these subtleties is likely to emerge clearly in the kinetics of a theatrical experience, and therefore they need all the more to be studied on the printed page.

Stage directions, when they appear at all in editions of Shakespeare plays, tend to be sparse, unlike the prolix passages in plays by authors like George Bernard Shaw. A lone reader may have trouble working out what needs to be done on stage with this terse direction for the trial scene: "Enter the Duke, the Magnificoes, Antonio, Bassanio, [Salerio] and Gratiano[with others]." Modern economic forces, like trade unions, have forced directors to limit the size of the court room assembly. Nowadays the old Elizabethan gimmick of employing only a handful of actors to represent dozens (a military siege managed by six soldiers) has resurfaced, though in the Radford film no expense seems to have been spared in filling a huge room in the Doge's Palace with hordes of richly costumed cast members.

Music often plays a role in establishing atmosphere in scenes like the choosing of the casket by Bassanio, which is either preceded or accompanied by a diegetic song, "Tell me where is fancy bred,/ Or in the heart or in the head" (3.2.63-64). The obvious rhyming of "bred" and "head" with "lead" hints at a deliberate move by Portia to move Bassanio toward the lead casket. If that is the case, however, such a cynical violation of sacred vows shatters her image as the perfect lady, and rings an alarm bell drawing attention to her Jekyll/Hyde persona. Directors have introduced the song in various ways, but none perhaps more startlingly than in Jonathan Miller's 1973 production, when two spinsterish looking ladies suddenly surface and erupt into the wildest but most compelling rendition imaginable. More generally the song functions like music for a sacred rite as in the carefully choreographed 2001 Nunn production when Portia kneels on a prayer cushion, her back ramrod straight, and crosses herself while Bassanio is choosing. Later, Portia will further demonstrate her steely inner reserves when she performs brilliantly as a pseudo-lawyer at Shylock's trial, and then, by the device of the ring scheme, manages to regain power over her fortune-hunting husband, Bassanio. There is yet another curious parallel in the play involving Portia with Jessica: Jessica defies Shylock, her miserly father, to run off with Lorenzo, a fortune hunter; Portia resents her father's role as a "control freak" and yearns for Bassanio, who is also, like Lorenzo, penniless. In the outcome, each young woman is stuck with a husband whom their fathers might have saved them from.

Readers thus become *de facto* directors, equipped to make intelligent decisions about the multiple ways for interpreting a Shakespearean text. The thoughtful reader will accumulate a set of opinions that may differ widely from what a director puts on stage. These ambiguities, however, are what after all make the works of William Shakespeare endlessly entertaining.

TIMELINE

400 AD: Residents of northeastern Italian towns are driven out by the Goths and seek refuge in the Venetian lagoon, whose hundred or more islands offered protection from mainland invaders.

March 25, 421: Venice formally founded, after invasions by Attila the Hun.

697: Venice is organized as a Republic under an elected Doge, which puts it centuries ahead of its time. Unfortunately, the greedy rich gradually converted the liberal political arrangement into an oligarchy.

828: Construction begins on St. Mark's Cathedral.

836: Venice undergoes serious attack by the Saracens.

874: The Bell Tower in St. Mark's Square is under construction

900: Hungarians attack Venice..

1071: The Doge's Palace is rebuilt after serious damage

1204: A split in the Ottoman empire allows Venice better access to the far east for prosperous trade in importing exotic eastern goods and exporting European products.

1450: Turkish invasion in which the Muslims sought to subdue the western Christians. Successfully opposed by the Holy Roman Empire, the Muslim hostility to the west has continued even into the 21st century, especially after the invasion of Iraq.

1558: Elizabeth I becomes the Queen of England

April 23, 1564. William Shakespeare christened at Trinity Church, Stratford, though it is assumed that he was born a few days before that.

1571: Naval Battle of Lepanto in the Bay of Corinth. Colossal fleets of eastern and western triremes, with hundreds of slaves laboring at the oars in the best Cecil B. DeMille tradition, turned the green sea red. After sickening casualties on both sides, the sailors of the Holy Roman Empire shattered the Turkish fleet, an event that Shakespeare incorporates into the background of *Othello*.

1582:   William Shakespeare marries Ann Hathaway. Their three children are Susannah (b.1583) and twins Hamnet and Judith (b. 1565). Hamnet dies in 1596.

1596:   *The Merchant of Venice*, otherwise called "The Jewe of Venyce," entered by James Robertes, printer, in Stationers' Register.

1598:   *The Merchant of Venice* probably acted at court.

1600:   Publication of *MV* Quarto version

1623:   Death of William Shakespeare in Stratford

Topics for Discussion and Further Study

Study Questions

1. What possible reasons are there for Antonio's sadness in the opening of the play? "In sooth I know not why I am so sad" (1.1.1.).How would a physician steeped in the doctrine of humours in Shakespeare's time have interpreted these symptoms? A modern psychiatrist?

2. The many references to the perils of the sea suggest a thematic link with the mercantile world of Venice. What does Gratiano mean when he says "they lose it that do buy it with much care" (1.1.75)? See also Matt. 16:26, "what shall it profit a man to gain the whole world and lose his own soul?"

3. How do Shylock's first lines in 1.3 characterize him? "Three thousand ducats—well." Is this obsessive or normal behavior?

4. How does the relationship between Launcelot Gobbo and his father in some respects echo the bond between Jessica and Shylock, Portia and her deceased father, Bassanio and Antonio?

5. Portia must deal with a character almost as exotic as Shylock in the person of Morocco. How does she handle him?

6. Each of the gold, silver and lead caskets carries a hidden lesson, which plays variations on the consequences of confusing appearance with reality, or to put it in a modern context, "You can't judge a book by its cover." What does the Moroccan's choice of the gold casket tell us about him?

7. In 2.9 after the Prince of Arragon has chosen the silver casket, what does Portia mean when she says "the candle sing'd the moth" (2.9.79).

8. At 3.1.43 Shylock suddenly erupts into his great speech "Hath not a Jew eyes...?..." which has becomes a timeless plea for tolerance. As you read the passage does it show that Shylock has turned away completely from his own bigotry, or does it leave him space to get even with his tormentors?

9. From a thematic standpoint, how can the abrupt shift in tone from the grim threat of bloodshed in the court room scene to the lyrical romanticism of the last act in Belmont be accounted for?

10. Is there anything about the historical events described in the love duet between Lorenzo and Jessica that suggests a harsh counterpoint to their own love affair? Do these blighted love affairs in any way portend the precarious outcome of a marriage based on disloyalty to parents?

11. Does Nerissa's love for Gratiano in any way implicitly comment on the love that Portia has for Bassanio?

Performance Questions

1. Is there a film version that compels you to feel more sympathetic toward Shylock? It has even been argued that Shylock's last line, "I am content," should be taken literally. Do the Shylocks of Laurence Olivier, Warren Mitchell, Henry Goodman, or Al Pacino seem "content" at the end of the trial scene? Is the fifth act designed to erase the ugliness of the fourth act?

2. Describe the ways in which Leah's ring is used in the Radford film to provide a sly commentary on the importance of the rings that Bassanio and Gratiano give to Portia and Nerissa.

3. In any film you have viewed is there a hint, or suggestion, that Portia violates, or yearns to violate her father's edict that she must be ruled by the man who chooses the proper casket? In what ways does "lead" coincide with the character of Bassanio?

4. Every director has a problem of what to do with Antonio at the end of the play when as a lonely bachelor, and even worse rejected by his friend Bassanio, he has no lover to be paired off with. In two or more films that you have seen describe how this final scene is handled.

5. Portia, who has been categorized by John Velz as an "Ovidian Grotesque," carries within herself, like Medea, a capacity to be either innocent or guileful. Imagine that you are casting a film of *Merchant* and select a contemporary actress that could manage this double-edged role.

6. The single stark opening line of the play, spoken by Antonio, leaves much room for thinking about the setting. How do you feel about Nunn's decision to open with a montage of events from the post-World War I era? Radford's extra-textual Jew-baiting on the Rialto? Jack Wise's use of a bare impressionistic garden setting?

7. If you were filming this play are there any episodes that you would wish to eliminate for social or political reasons, and if so how would you justify your decision?

8. The Jack Wise BBC version and the Trevor Nunn television productions serve as fine examples of a conservative (old fashioned) as compared with a liberal ("cool") approach to staging Shakespeare. Compare them from the standpoint of casting, costuming, settings, and elocution.

BIBLIOGRAPHY

Barnet, Sylvan, Ed. *Twentieth Century Interpretations of* The Merchant of Venice:. *A Collection of Critical Essays*. Englewood Cliffs (New Jersey): Prentice- Hall, 1970.

> Although compiled three decades ago before the great wave of European theory, there is a much worthwhile material in this anthology. For example, C.L. Barber's "The Merchant and the Jew of Venice" looks at the ideological gap in the trial scene between Shylock and Portia, who in many ways embody Old and New Testament values; and G. Wilson Knight's "The Ideal Production" spells out key contrasts between the commercial world of Venice and the "spelled" land of Belmont.

Bevington, David. *How to Read a Shakespeare Play*. Oxford: Blackwell Publishing, 2006.

> Advice from a prominent editor of Shakespeare's plays about how best to read them.

Bulman, James. *Shakespeare in Performance*. The Merchant of Venice. London and Manchester: Manchester UP, 1991.

> James Bulman undertakes the enormous job of tracing productions of the *Merchant* from the Jacobean period to modern times. His special achievement lies in the interweaving of social and cultural history with staging decor. Especially helpful is the section on Russian director Theodore Komisarjevsky who pioneered in putting Shakespeare into the context of emerging twentieth-century art. With his Marxist point of view, he toppled the plays from their Victorian roles as praetorians of establishment tastes, and introduced to the stage Italian *Commedia* motifs as well as Picasso and cubism.

Chambers, E.K. *William Shakespeare: A Study of Facts and Problems*, I. Oxford: Clarendon Press, 1930: 368-74.

> The definitive summary of the facts (just the facts—no attempt to be clever) surrounding *The Merchant of Venice,* not likely to be improved upon.

Crowl, Samuel. "Looking for Shylock: Stephen Greenblatt, Michael Radford, and Al Pacino." In *Screening Shakespeare in the Twenty-First Century.* Eds. Mark Thornton Burnett and Ramona Wray. Edinburgh: Edinburgh UP, 2006: 113-26.

Samuel Crowl's important essay uses contemporary film and literary theory to insert Radford's film of *The Merchant* into its full context. Radford's close shots of Jessica's turquoise ring show how the film expands on Shylock's grief over the loss of Leah's ring and becomes an image of Jessica's own deep remorse.

Danson, Lawrence. *The Harmonies of* The Merchant of Venice. New Haven and London: Yale UP, 1978.

A clever, even light-hearted writer, Danson plunges into the maelstrom of *Merchant* narratives to identify "harmonies" in the midst of the play's obvious disharmonies. In discussing the difficult issue of Shylock, the one great subverter in the play, Danson makes the point that "…the fact that the moneylender's services were nonetheless indispensable must have made the problem seem quite literally diabolical" (144).

Edelman, Charles, Ed. *Shakespeare in Production.* The Merchant of Venice. Cambridge: Cambridge UP, 2002.

Edelman's book is "scholarly" in the sense that it covers the history of *The Merchant* on stage in a thorough and unassuming way. It also offers a readable commentary, often illustrated with scenes from productions under discussion. Generous materials in the appendices give outlines of stage history with dates, names of directors, principal actors, and venues. There are also appendices on Shylock and Jessica's duet of the Hebrew "Eshet Chavil," as well as a discusssion of how in nineteenth-century theater, when the verbose Morocco and Arragon were eliminated from the play, elements of their casket speeches were transposed into Bassanio's lines.

Gilbert, Miriam. *Shakespeare at Stratford.* The Merchant of Venice. Stratford-upon-Avon: Shakespeare Birthplace Trust and the Arden Shakespeare, 2002.

Detailed essays on the ways that *The Merchant* has been presented in Stratford by the Royal Shakespeare Company. For example, a close descriptions of the scenes in Belmont during the selection of the caskets includes the 1971 production with Judi Dench as Portia and Ultz's 1984 production with levitated caskets adding drama to the choice of metals. Gilbert stresses the ambiguity of how extensive Portia's knowledge was of the caskets, and whether or not she cheated her father, for which there are no answers, only puzzles.

Halio, Jay. The Merchant of Venice. *The Oxford Shakespeare*. Oxford: The Clarendon Press, 1993.

Halio carries the study of the play's permutations and combinations into the twentieth century where he shows particular sensitivity to the radical 1932 Komisarjevsky production that brought the whole Pandora's box of irony and socialist ideology into Shakespearean theater. To Komisarjevsky, *The Merchant* was "a fantastic comedy to be staged as such."

Lake, James H. "The Influence of Primacy and Recency upon Audience Responses to Michael Radford's *The Merchant of Venice*." Publication forthcoming.

Magnus, Laury. "Michael Radford's *The Merchant of Venice* and the Vexed Question of Performance." *Literature/Film Quarterly* 35.2 (2007): 108-20.

Magnus cites the history of hostility to *The Merchant* for its alleged anti-Semitism and shows how Radford's close shot of Jessica's ring at the end of the movie steers the film away from festive comedy toward a more meditative experience.

Mahon, John W. and Ellen Mcleod Mahon, Eds. The Merchant of Venice: *New Critical Essays*. New York and London: Routledge, 2002.

Essays that collectively reclaim the status of *Merchant* as a play of extraordinary complexity that richly deserves fresh examination every five decades or so. R.W. Desai in his "Mislike Me Not for My Complexion" shows how Portia's treatment of the suitors masks her personal insecurities; Karoline Szatek in "The Politics of Commerce" exposes Portia's Belmont as not entirely a "green world" innocent of the commercial values of Venice; and Grace Tiffany unfolds a fascinating panoply built on the names of the characters: Antonio, for example, as derived from Antonio da Ponte, the builder of Venice's Rialto bridge; and John W. Velz on "Portia and the Ovidian Grotesque," enough to keep anyone busy reading and thinking for years. Among all these brilliant essays, editor John W. Mahon's Herculean contribution in tracing four centuries of criticism and commentary on *The Merchant* provides a stiff backbone for the entire anthology.

Mahood, M.M., Ed. *The Merchant of Venice*. Cambridge: Cambridge UP, 2003,

According to Mahood, sailing ships are "an unseen presence throughout the play," a key clue being the reference to the "wealthy Andrew," purportedly a Spanish naval vessel originally christened San Andrés that was captured at Cadiz, These and other insights help to establish the social context in which the play was written and deepen understanding of Antonio's anxieties about his sea-borne investments.

Marcus, Leah S., Ed. *William Shakespeare.* The Merchant of Venice. *A Norton Critical Edition: Authoritative Text, Source and Contexts, Criticism. Rewritings and Appropriations.* New York and London: W.W. Norton & Company, 2006.

A marvelous array of essays by distinguished writers, including Sigmund Freud on "The Theme of the Three Caskets," James Shapiro on "Circumcision and the 'Pound of Flesh'," and Abraham Oz, "*The Merchant of Venice* in Israel."

Rothwell, Kenneth S. "Trevor Nunn's *The Merchant of Venice*: Portia's House of Mystery, Magic, and Menace," in *Acts of Criticism: Performance Matters in Shakespeare and His Contemporaries. Essays in Honor of James P. Lusardi,* Eds. Paul Nelsen and June Schlueter. Madison/Teaneck: Fairleigh Dickinson UP, 2006: 204-16.

Using the deceptive appearance of the three caskets as a basis, Rothwell tries to show that the question of appearance vs. reality is the underlying theme that unites all the plot lines in the play.

Silverstone, Catherine. "Speaking Māori Shakespeare: *The Maori Merchant of Venice* and the Legacy of Colonisation" in *Screening Shakespeare in the Twenty-First Century.* Eds. Mark Thornton Burnett and Ramona Wray. Edinburgh: Edinburgh UP, 2006: 127-45.

Anyone interested in the genesis and production of *The Merchant of Venice* in the context of New Zealand's aboriginal culture will find this well researched contribution rewarding..

FILMOGRAPHY

Le miroir de Venise: Une mesaventure de Shylock. France 1902. Dir. Georges Méliès. Silent/b&w. Runtime 2 mins.

    Innovative film maker and inventor Georges Méliès was also a pioneer in the production of Shakespeare movies, though it has been argued that he sometimes used only the title and little else.

The Merchant of Venice. USA 1908. Dir. William Ranous w. Julia Gordon (Portia). Silent/tinted. Runtime 10 mins.

    One of a dozen truncated Shakespeare movies filmed in Brooklyn at the Flatbush studio of the Vitagraph company. Its director, William Ranous, was a Broadway actor recruited by J. Stuart Blackton, former Edison associate and Vitagraph mogul. The jumpiness and nervousness of these one-reel Shakespeare movies came partly from an industry bias against longer movies, sometimes from variations in the speed of projection, and often from the primitive equipment.

Il Mercante di Venezia. Italy 1910 . Dir. Gerolamo Savio w. Ermete Novelli. (Shylock), Francesca Bertini (Portia). b&w. DVD "Silent Shakespeare." Milestone Film and Video. Runtime 8 mins.

    The plot line is skewed to make Jessica and Lorenzo more prominent than in Shakespeare's script, yet the striking exterior shots of Venice's canals and bridges go far beyond the crudities of the Flatbush movies. Francesca Bertini makes an energetic but frumpy Portia.

Shylock, ou le mercante de Venise. France 1913. Dir. Henri Desfontaines w. Harry Baur (Shylock), Pepe Bonafé (Portia). Silent/b&w. English subtitles. Runtime 33 mins.

    A leap ahead as the art of storytelling in film began to profit from new techniques more adequate for Shakespeare. The choosing of the caskets in Portia's posh Belmont villa is carried out with particular élan.

The Merchant of Venice. UK 1916. Dir.Walter West w. Matheson Lang (Shylock), Hutin Britton (Portia). Silent /b&w. Runtime 21 mins.

The entire ensemble at London's St. James Theatre was dragooned into putting a Shakespeare play on screen "as is." How "as is" may never be known since an extant print at the Folger Shakespeare library abruptly terminates in the middle of the trial scene. Lang's Shylock shows a humanitarian side to soften the popular image of a crass villain.

Der Kaufmann von Venedig, The Jew of Mestri. Germany 1923/26. Dir. Peter Paul Felner w. Werner Krauss (Shylock) and Henny Porten (Portia). Runtime 64 mins.

Traces of German expressionism identify this successful film as a product of the post-WWI Weimar period. A 1926 re-release brought the film to North America.

The Merchant of Venice. UK 1947. Dir. George More O'Ferrall w. Abraham Sofaer (Shylock), Margaretta Scott (Portia), Jill Balcon (Jessica). BBC TV, Tuesday evening 1 July 1947. Runtime 127 mins.

For 1947 this was a very ambitious television program, which emerged under the directorship of George More O'Ferrall, a leader in the re-emergence of British television after a wartime hiatus.

The Merchant of Venice. UK 1955. Dir. Hal Burton w. Rachel Gurney (Portia), Veronica Wells (Jessica), Michael Hordern (Shylock). BBC Television, Sunday evening March 13, 1955. Runtime 120 mins.

An established actor like Michael Hordern as Shylock shed an aura of dignity to Shakespeare on television but the critics were unmerciful. The (London) *Times* critic hated the idea of Shakespeare on television and launched a diatribe against the pretense that the audience was being allowed to watch a performance at the Globe.

The Merchant of Venice, UK 1969; USA 1974. Dir Jonathan Miller w. Laurence Olivier (Shylock), Joan Plowright (Portia), Anthony Nicholls (Antonio). BBC Television. USA/ABC 8:30 P.M. to 11 P.M., March 16, 1974. VHS/ DVD. Runtime 150 mins.

Laurence Olivier's fastidious performance as Shylock, updated into an Edwardian businessman, has put this production in the forefront of *Merchant* performance history. His anguish while saying "I am content"at the end of the trial makes it apparent that Shylock is anything but content.

The Merchant of Venice UK 1980. Dir. Jack Gold, w. Warren Mitchell (Shylock), Gemma Jones (Portia), John Franklyn-Robbins (Antonio). BBC/Time-Life (The Shakespeare Plays series). USA Public Television, Feb. 23, 1981. VHS/DVD. Runtime 169 mins.

A quarter of a century later this production takes on a "dated" look, mainly in the noticeable stinginess of the sets and the cramped camera style that records set speeches by talking heads rather than live interaction among the actors. A great exception is Warren Mitchell who conveys the subtlety of Shylock's mind through brilliant voice and gesture.

The Merchant of Venice. "A Taste of Shakespeare" 1995. Dir. Eric Weinthal w. Brian Tree (Shylock), Richard McMillan (Antonio), Stuart Hughes (Bassanio), Ann-Marie MacDonald (Portia). Eugenia Educational Foundation. Bullfrog Films. Runtime 51 mins.

A videotape intended for high school and college students. Actors tell the story of a specific play, act out a scene, and comment on it.

The Merchant of Venice. UK 2001. Dir. Trevor Nunn w. Henry Goodman (Shylock), Derbhle Crotty (Portia), David Bamber (Antonio). Royal Natonal Theatre. Image Entertainment DVD 141 mins.

Widely acclaimed as a triumph, this television performance includes a brilliant performance by Derbhle Crotty who plays Portia as the ice princess of Belmont. Putting the action into the decadence of 1930s Berlin and turning Belmont into a minimalist retreat, Nunn manages to retain the play's spirit while sacrificing many lines to the tyranny of television time.

The Merchant of Venice. USA/UK/ Luxembourg/ Italy, 2004. Dir. Michael Radford, w. Al Pacino (Shylock), Joseph Fiennes (Bassanio), Jeremy Irons (Antonio), Lynn Collins (Portia). Sony Pictures DVD. Runtime 131mins.

The most expensive film ever made of the *Merchant* with opulent costumes and sets and plentiful use of the architectural treasures of Venice itself. Eager to put the play into its historical context, Radford's Shylock as superbly played by Al Pacino becomes as much a victim as a villain.